What People Are Saying about *Moving*

As a new nonprofit executive director, I f
invaluable guide to this complex and ch
articulates the many roles and responsib
illustrates them with stories from her ow
read for any new or aspiring executive director!

Deirdre M. Gelinne, Executive Director
Westfield United Fund

This book is a truly important contribution that defines how nonprofit leaders can build lasting accomplishments and success for their organizations.

Chris Sienkielewski, President
Three Bridges LLC

It is one thing to aspire; it is another to achieve. Moving Up *could be the pathway to connecting aspiration with achievement for those beginning the journey of being "in charge" of a nonprofit. Must reading.*

Sidney Blanchard, Executive Director
Community Access Unlimited

Moving Up *is an excellent, step-by-step, resource for anyone preparing to take on an executive leadership position in the nonprofit arena, as well as for seasoned executive directors who may be struggling with financial concerns, balancing the limitless demands of running a nonprofit, or needing advice on working with their board.*

Beth Blakey, President
ReWrite Consulting

Joanne's guide for new executive directors, Moving Up, *is a breath of fresh air for nonprofit leaders. She offers practical advice for new and seasoned CEOs alike, making her guide a training school for new puppies and for old dogs wanting to learn new tricks. As one of the old dogs, I have found new insights, practical tips, and refreshing reminders for everyday use. This is a terrific, useful read, and I highly recommend it to emerging and experienced nonprofit leaders alike.*

Bill Webb, Executive Director
Family and Children's Services

Joanne Oppelt has delivered a deeply researched, smoothly organized, and well-written primer on nonprofit management. Moving Up *deserves a home in the desk of every new nonprofit executive.*

Maureen Tinen, President
UCEDC

Moving Up to Executive Director: Lessons Learned from My First 365 Days

One of the **In the Trenches**™ series

Published by
CharityChannel Press, an imprint of CharityChannel LLC
30021 Tomas, Suite 300
Rancho Santa Margarita, CA 92688-2128 USA

charitychannel.com

ISBN Print Book: 978-1-938077-09-8 | ISBN eBook: 978-1-938077-29-6

Library of Congress Control Number: 2013935861

13 12 11 10 9 8 7 6 5 4 3 2 1

Printed in the United States of America

Moving Up to Executive Director

Lessons Learned from My First 365 Days

Joanne Oppelt, MHA, GPC

CharityChannel®
PRESS™

Publisher's Acknowledgments

This book was produced by a team dedicated to excellence; please send us your feedback to editors@charitychannel.com.

We first wish to acknowledge the tens of thousands of peers who call charitychannel.com their online professional home. Your enthusiastic support for the **In the Trenches™** series is the wind in our sails.

Members of the team who produced this book include:

Editors

Acquisitions Editor: Linda Lysakowski

Comprehensive Editor: Joshua Baxt

Copy Editor: Stephen Nill

Production

In the Trenches Series Design: Deborah Perdue

Layout Editor: Jill McLain

Proofreaders: Joshua Baxt, Linda Lysakowski, Jill McLain, Stephen Nill

Administrative

CharityChannel LLC: Stephen C. Nill, CEO

Marketing and Public Relations: John Millen

About the Author

Joanne Oppelt has been improving organizational bottom lines since 1993. Currently Executive Director at CONTACT We Care, in Westfield, New Jersey, Joanne manages day-to-day agency operations, develops and monitors budgets, increases net revenues, and oversees organizational marketing and resource development. She is also an adjunct professor at Kean University, where she teaches nonprofit management and fund development.

As Development Director at Community Access Unlimited for nine years, Joanne personally raised more than $9.3 million through government, corporate, foundation, and individual support, increasing agency annual operating revenues by more than $1.75 million. She also reduced costs by more than a hundred thousand dollars by negotiating strategic vendor relationships. In addition, Joanne created the agency's corporate marketing materials and instituted the CAU Community Network.

During her tenure at Prevent Child Abuse New Jersey, Joanne oversaw a $1.2 million U.S. Department of Education grant. She formed a statewide Parental Assistance Advisory Committee, uniting groups with competing agendas to achieve a common goal. She also garnered national and state recognition for the organization as the NJ Parents As Teachers State Coordinating Agency.

While at the March of Dimes, Joanne facilitated the funding allocation process through the volunteer Health Professionals Advisory Committee. She also facilitated the volunteer Community Health Education Committee, implementing professional education conferences and increasing volunteer participation in the Babies and You Speakers Bureau by 200 percent.

Joanne's previous books include *Power Your Organization's Fundraising: How the Partnership Paradigm Will Change Everything; Succeed in Your Nonprofit Funding Partnerships: Analyzing Their Costs and Benefits;* and *Confessions of a Successful Grants Writer: A Complete Guide to Discovering and Obtaining Funding.*

Joanne holds a Bachelors of Arts in Education from Bethany University in Santa Cruz, California and a Masters in Health Administration from Wilkes University in Wilkes-Barre, Pennsylvania.

She lives in New Jersey with her husband Rick.

Author's Acknowledgments

My first thanks go to my board: Karen, Jeffrey, Russ, Geoff, Howie, Leesa, Bob, JoAnn, Susan, and Nancy—who provided wisdom and guidance during my first year as a novice executive director. I thank you for your faith in me. I thank you for this and for your unfailing support. We have come together as a team and accomplished so much. Your leadership and willingness to do the hard work has put us where we are today.

I also thank my volunteers, without whose labors of love CONTACT would cease to exist. You are on the front lines and are our lifeblood. Your passion and constancy amaze me.

I specifically want to thank Sue Fasano, my director of programs. Sue, you were the stalwart of consistency during all the transitions before I came. You are proficient at what you do and a valuable member of my team. You make it rewarding to come to the office every day.

And my thanks to Sid Blanchard and Bill Webb, my colleagues and friends. Thank you for listening to me and showing me how it's done. I admire both of you.

My gratitude also goes out to my book reviewers: Chris Reardon, Karen Yutsus, Fran McTernan, and Sue Fasano. Thank you for your feedback.

And thank you to the CharityChannel team: Linda Lysakowski, my editor and Stephen Nill, my publisher. I am humbled to learn from your experiences and take advantage of your accomplishments. I am honored you consider me one of your colleagues.

As always, my deepest thanks go to my husband, who stands by me through the ups and downs, successes and failures, joys and challenges. Rick, you are my bedrock. I am blessed to have you as my mate and companion. You make me a better person.

Thank you all for what you offer and what you have given. You all truly make my life worth living.

Contents

Summary of Chapters

Chapter One: Preparing for Executive Leadership. Chapter One dives into the skills needed for executive leadership. What do executive recruiters look for in executive director candidates? I also include real-life stories about how four executive directors acclimated to their positions and what prepared them for the challenges. The chapter concludes by examining the commonalities in each executive director's experiences.

Chapter Two: You Got the Job! Now What? Chapter Two explores the excitement and awe of taking on executive director responsibilities. I discuss the importance of celebrating successes, as well as making unpopular decisions. I also talk about developing peer and professional support systems to help guide you through new situations.

Chapter Three: You Getting to Know Them—Them Getting to Know You. In Chapter Three, I talk about the honeymoon—that period of unusual harmony when a relationship first begins. I also discuss the tensions when you get to know each other a little better as the honeymoon ends, and the joys of developing the relationship.

Chapter Four: Working with the Board. Chapter Four examines the complexity of defining executive director/board roles and responsibilities. The chapter also probes the importance of the executive director/board president relationship and the challenge of managing group dynamics.

Chapter Five: When Everything Demands Your Attention. Being an executive director is a big job with multiple priorities. Chapter Five delves into structuring a manageable workload. I discuss balancing external and internal priorities, as well as long- and short-term goals. I finish with a discussion about delegating to others.

Chapter Six: Financial Management. Money management is a reflection of values and should always be done with the mission in mind. In Chapter Six, I cover how I manage revenue, expenses, and cash flow. I also talk about financial management concepts that help me get the most bang for my buck.

Chapter Seven: Resource Development. Chapter Seven underscores the importance of putting mission first when raising funds, ways to diversify revenue and creating a revenue generation plan. I also discuss the role the executive director plays in fundraising and how everyone in the organization is a fundraiser.

Chapter Eight: Working with Staff and Volunteers. Chapter Eight articulates the importance of clearly defined (paid and unpaid) staff roles and responsibilities, what motivates staff and volunteers, staff development methods, and the value of open communication.

Chapter Nine: Working with the Community. Chapter Nine focuses on uniting the community to meet shared needs, the purpose of nonprofits and their accountability to the community. The chapter also talks about ways to collaborate with different types of community agencies.

Chapter Ten: Building for the Future. Chapter Ten develops the planning to plan concept, i.e., laying the foundation for strategic planning. I cover how I laid both the operational and financial foundations on which future decisions are built. I also discuss how playing off my base motivators helps me plan. The chapter ends by exploring both the good and bad consequences of growth.

Chapter Eleven: Personal Development. Chapter Eleven begins by talking about the role executive leaders' personal value systems play in creating corporate cultures. I then turn to the importance of self-awareness and underscore the value of self-confidence. Finally, I describe different paths to personal development.

Chapter Twelve: Work/Life Balance. I end the book with a chapter on work/life balance, a notorious shortcoming for executive directors. I talk about scheduling personal time, engaging in self-care activities, and tapping into personal support systems.

Foreword

Moving Up to Executive Director: Lessons Learned from My First 365 Days is a must-read for anyone in the nonprofit sector—particularly newly appointed chief executive officers and those aspiring to this crucial position. The volunteer board members who work with new executive directors in America's growing nonprofit sector will also benefit from this book. Studies have estimated that nearly 75 percent of current nonprofit executive directors plan to retire in the next five to ten years. With an estimated 1.5 million nonprofit organizations in the country (according to the National Center for Charitable Statistics), a leadership vacuum for thousands of organizations is nearly upon us.

While this increase in executive turnover may threaten nonprofit sector sustainability, it also creates an opportunity for emerging leaders to develop new skills and knowledge to successfully guide their organizations into the future. Speaking as the founder and Executive Director of Fairleigh Dickinson University's Center for Excellence: Leadership, Governance, and Philanthropy, today's emerging leaders will greatly benefit from Joanne's book on "the new executive director's guide to leading a nonprofit."

At a time when thousands of individuals will be assuming the executive leadership position in their organizations, Joanne's book provides an outstanding comprehensive guide to understand and prepare those new to executive leadership for their role and responsibilities.

Having known Joanne Oppelt for many years, I am happy to say she is fully qualified to undertake this important work. Joanne's personal experience is on display in each chapter, as she skillfully describes the personal and professional struggles that have shaped her own career. She artfully provides real-life practical experiences in dealing with each subject, ranging from preparing for the executive leadership role and working with the board and community, to dealing with the demands of the job, personal development and how to balance life and work—something everyone in leadership struggles with at times.

Through my work over the past thirty years as a chief executive officer and board chair, as well as an experienced author, speaker, and strategic advisor to hundreds of nonprofit organizations in the United States, I have found Joanne Oppelt's *Moving Up to Executive Director: Lessons Learned from My First 365 Days* a terrific work, filled with practical advice, shared experiences, and suggestions. I highly recommend that you read this book.

Dennis C. Miller

Executive Director
Fairleigh Dickinson University's Center for Excellence: Leadership, Governance and Philanthropy

President & CEO
Dennis C. Miller Associates, Inc.
Strategic Advisors to the Nonprofit Community
www.dcmillerassociates.com

Introduction

On Monday, August 29, 2011, I was offered the executive director position at a small community nonprofit in New Jersey. I was excited about beginning this new chapter in my life and looking forward to the challenge of leading the small agency into its next stage of development. I had been looking for new challenges for a while. I was thrilled, excited, and a little anxious about what lay ahead of me. But I liked exploring new territory and expanding my horizons and (I thought) knew that I was ready for what I was getting into. Little did I know how right and wrong my perceptions were, and how prepared and unprepared I was for the challenges I was about to take on.

This book is written for anyone who wants to become an executive director, understand what it takes to transition into an executive leadership position, or become better prepared to handle executive responsibilities. *Moving Up to Executive Director: Lessons Learned from My First 365 Days* is written from my perspective as a lifelong nonprofit professional with a master's degree in health administration. I started in program development and moved into fundraising before landing in the corner office.

My personal history and struggles have shaped who I am and my opportunities to create my own future. I try to present the concepts that have affected me most and have the most universal application. My ultimate goal is to make this book real, relatable, and applicable.

Each chapter will begin with a bulleted overview of its main concepts, followed by a brief introduction. Throughout the chapter, you will find sidebars that add detail to the narrative, give hints on applying the principles being discussed or tell real-life experiences, followed by suggestions based on the chapter's subject matter.

I am only one executive director at one agency in one corner of the world. I do not have all the answers. None of us does. But as I share my experiences, strengths, challenges, and successes with you, I hope that you gain some knowledge of what executive leadership takes, the skills you might need to take on an executive position, or how to support someone going through their own executive transition. I hope that you glean some insights from my achievements and challenges that you can apply to your own situations.

Best of luck as you move forward in your career.

Chapter One

Preparing for Executive Leadership

IN THIS CHAPTER

- What executive recruiters look for
- The real-world scoop
- Putting it all together

August 29, 2011, that was the day I was offered my executive director position. I was excited about the possibilities that lay ahead of me. I was honored by the trust the board of directors had placed in me and a little anxious about the transition before me. What prepared me most for the executive director role? How did I get there? What challenges was I unprepared for?

In this chapter, I begin the executive director journey with an overview of the skills and characteristics recruiters look for in executive director candidates. I also relate how four seasoned executive directors rose to the executive suite: what prepared them best for their roles, what they found most helpful going into the role and what they found most challenging about the job. One of them moved up within her own organization. One took on increasing responsibility at different organizations in the same field. One moved up through progressive leadership positions in different organizations in different fields. And one founded the organization. Whatever your path to executive leadership, my hope is you find wisdom in their experiences.

What Executive Recruiters Look For

Executive directors need to be proficient in many areas and possess many outstanding qualities. One executive recruiter outlined the skills and characteristics that she looks for in executive director candidates in terms of specific technical proficiencies:

- finance
- operations
- technology
- project management
- strategic planning
- marketing
- human resources
- compliance

In addition, she also looks for a variety of soft skills:

- outstanding personal dexterity
- self-awareness
- thoughtful communication
- analytical and creative problem-solving
- collaboration
- openness

> The executive director is the chief executive officer of a company, organization, or corporation, particularly a nonprofit. The executive director designs, develops, and implements strategic plans for the organization in a cost-effective and time-efficient manner, as well as managing the organization's day-to-day operations. The board grants the executive director authority to manage the organization.
>
> Executive leadership is characterized by the ability to build trust with others, communicate well, work collaboratively, manage risk, solve problems creatively, influence and inspire colleagues, provide professional development, and continuously seek improvement.
>
> definition

- a high degree of emotional intelligence
- mutual respect
- concern for others
- integrity

Obviously, being an executive director is a big job. You need expertise in a wide variety of fields, are expected to perform well in many spheres, and must function well with multiple and diverse constituencies. (I talk more about executive director job descriptions in **Chapter Five**.) Executive leadership is a lot to take on.

The Real-World Scoop

The following stories are based on interviews with current executive directors. Rather than tell you how they successfully manage their organizations, these stories show how they managed their *transitions* to the executive director role. Each executive has a different story, with different training, background, management style, strengths, and weaknesses.

Pat's Story

The first thing you notice about Pat is her passion for her work. Her excitement is contagious. Pat is driven by mission to serve families. Everything she does is guided by her organization's impact on the lives of the families with whom it works. You cannot talk to Pat without getting excited about her agency's work.

> An organization's mission is its reason for being. A mission statement is an articulation of what the organization is and why it exists, defining the organization's primary clients, identifying the products and services the agency offers, and describing the geographical location where it operates.
>
> definition

Pat works in early childhood education. She started with her organization as a program assistant, eventually rising to executive director. When the previous executive director moved on and the board began its search for new leadership, Pat asked to be considered for the position. With a nine-year tenure at the agency, Pat felt she knew the organization inside and out and could contribute at a higher level.

Pat has no advanced degree in education or administration. She comes from the school of real-life experience. At first, Pat felt intimidated by her peers, who had more formal academic training. She felt small compared to the Ph.D.'s so common in educational leadership. But she soon realized that her life experience had prepared her for the challenges of being an executive director at a small nonprofit. She found that she was just as rooted as her peers.

Before entering the nonprofit world, Pat helped run a family business. She was skilled in sales and marketing, bookkeeping, payroll, human resources, and audits. Her voice is strong and steady as she emphasizes the value of her experiences managing a small business. Many of the same administrative skills are required to run a small nonprofit.

> Pat's previous experience running a small business was invaluable in preparing her for executive director responsibilities.
>
> **observation**

Pat realizes she is not an expert on everything. For example, with an endowment to manage, Pat recognizes she is not an investment policy expert. But she knows other people who are and taps into their strengths. Each time an organizational weakness is identified, Pat finds someone with expertise in that area. As a result, people know how they can best contribute and find fulfillment working from their strengths. Her volunteers, including her board, are adept at their work and dedicated to the organization. These strengths are good for them, good for Pat, good for the organization, and good for the children served by the organization.

Pat inherited a $500,000 budget, two staff (including her) and about a hundred twenty-five volunteers. Ninety-six percent of her revenues come from community contributions, mainly foundations. About 3 percent is income from an endowment and 1 percent comes from program fees.

Pat finds mastering information is her most valuable skill. She likes to have data at her fingertips, particularly donor data, and likes having ready answers for her board. She encourages all executive directors understand their information systems' capabilities, especially their software. She believes in using information to its fullest potential.

The most challenging part of Pat's transition to executive director was learning how to manage volunteers, which she had never done before. It took some time for her to learn how to best utilize them, setting up organizational structures that would work for her and her unpaid staff.

> Pat uses the power of information to its full potential.
>
> **observation**

Scheduling is a good example. To work with volunteers, and provide the oversight they want, she expects them to work when she needs them, rather than anytime they offer. She had to learn how to communicate expectations and limits and still motivate the people who wanted to give to her organization. She considers working with volunteers a crucial skill to lead a nonprofit.

You can hear the fondness in Pat's voice as she talks about her volunteers and board members. She sees herself as a co-worker and colleague, not as someone wielding leadership power to do things her way. Her role is to get rid of the power relationship and work collaboratively with others.

As a result, Pat enjoys a very harmonious relationship with her board and volunteers. All her board members are upfront, with no hidden agendas. "I have the greatest board," she says. "People genuinely want the children to thrive."

Pat's greatest joy as an executive director is hearing from parents whose children are being given opportunities they would not otherwise have. These opportunities pay off by improving the children's education and their lives.

She also enjoys working with other organizations. She is proud of her agency's ability to establish partnerships with a wide variety of community agencies, including schools, shelters, food pantries, medical providers, and government agencies. She values the services other agencies offer her clients and community. As she works with them, she appreciates that her organization is a part of an overall spectrum of services. She treasures her agency's role as part of the greater community.

at believes success as an executive director stems from her passion for the mission and willingness to roll up your sleeves and work. She finds it very rewarding to keep children in school, make sure her organization has money in the bank, and maintain a strong relationship with her board. "It is an amazing feeling to be a changing force," she states.

> "It is an amazing feeling to be a changing force."
>
> Pat

Because of her agency's size, previous executive directors had used the position as a stepping stone to bigger organizations with more responsibilities and higher incomes. But, so far, not Pat. She loves her job and is happy where she is. Pat is extremely fulfilled by her role—changing young lives for the better.

Gerry's Story

Gerry has always been interested in child welfare. With a bachelor's in sociology and a master's in social work, his passion for children and youth influences everything he does. Through direct mental health and family services, Gerry develops systems to help children and youth thrive.

Before pursuing executive leadership, Gerry was a licensed clinician and community planner. To move up the ladder, while maintaining his involvement with kids, Gerry took positions with increasing responsibility at different agencies in different states. He was interested in pursuing executive leadership, both to grow an organization and move up the income ladder.

Gerry's experiences as a community planner have helped him handle his executive director responsibilities. He gets excited when talking about his exposure to social and support services, both as a volunteer and a professional. He also relishes his experience developing a community-wide needs assessment. Running meetings helped him as well, giving him a taste of group dynamics and providing good practice for board meetings.

His work in program planning and proposal writing has also been invaluable. These disciplines help him understand the organization's big picture while maintaining mastery over the details. This grant-writing perspective helps him understand his community, garner revenue, and develop evaluation metrics for the programs he implements.

Gerry is grateful for his education in human development and dynamics. He becomes animated when discussing interpersonal interactions. To succeed, an executive director needs to accept people where they are and embrace their differences. Understanding what connects people has a multiplier effect, increasing the impact of individuals and organizations. In addition, Gerry has deep respect for other organizations in his community. By tapping into the energy produced by people and organizations, he accomplishes the mission and satisfies all constituencies—board, staff, and community.

> Gerry's experience in program planning and proposal writing was invaluable in taking on the executive director role.
>
> **observation**

"Executive directors need to be proficient managers," says Gerry. "Successful executive directors must maintain a passion for their organization's mission and see the big picture, as well as the details."

These perspectives have been crucial, helping Gerry design and implement programs and find revenue to sustain them. Gerry relies heavily on his ability to analyze the interventions he proposes, down to the smallest detail.

The most important hard skill for would-be executives to master is organizational metrics—the numbers. For Gerry, using organizational metrics effectively means understanding financial statements, as well as evaluating outcomes, developing a deep understanding of the data required to assess organizational performance and using those numbers to advance the mission.

When he first became executive director, Gerry's biggest challenge was managing the transition. His board, staff, and volunteers were used to a different leadership style. Each group had different needs and Gerry had to figure out how to manage those differences. He had to blend competing priorities and perspectives.

> Understand the data required to assess organizational performance and use those numbers to advance the mission.
>
> **practical tip**

The most unpleasant part of Gerry's job is addressing staff and volunteer performance issues, which can generate unpopular decisions. Gerry has uncovered staff that were not doing their jobs and even fabricating reports. When the culprits were held in high esteem, he would be pressured to excuse their actions and tolerate their behavior for the sake of the community. Gerry took the high road and set boundaries. In the short term, consequences were not pleasant. But in the long term, Gerry developed a better functioning organization.

Gerry's advice to new executive directors is to make sure you understand and embrace the mission of the organization you will be leading and the organizational foundation you've inherited. Don't come in with guns blazing to make an immediate mark. Get to know the organization and its strengths. Learn the history first and meet the organization where it is.

> Make sure you understand and embrace the mission and foundational strengths of the organization you will be leading.
>
> practical tip

Gerry's greatest joy as an executive director is developing effective programs and new, creative ways to deliver services. He enjoys working with all kinds of people in different capacities—clients, staff, volunteers, donors, funders, and legislators—to make things work right. He is a man with a mission, garnering human potential to fulfill that mission.

Robyn's Story

In graduate school, Robyn, who has a master's in social work, took a course in nonprofit administration because so many practitioners end up in administrative positions. Though it didn't provide much preparation to enter the executive suite, it was at least a start. Robyn moved from a lower level administrative leadership position to a higher level position in a different organization and in a different field, but in the same region.

Prior to becoming an executive director, Robyn was a department director at a medium-sized, professionally staffed, mainly government-funded nonprofit helping people with disabilities. She had budget responsibilities; managed her department's employees (including hiring and firing); and networked with community partners. Robyn sought an executive director position because she wanted more autonomy.

When she took over a large, volunteer-led agency helping children develop into responsible adults, Robyn inherited fifteen staff members, three thousand volunteers, and a $1.2 million budget. Much of her time was spent managing volunteers. Most of her revenue (60 percent) came from product sales. She also had a healthy revenue stream (35 percent) from program fees. Other income sources were minor.

As executive director, one of the first things Robyn did was take advantage of the training offered by her organization's national office. With only one graduate class in nonprofit administration under her belt, Robyn felt she needed more formal education in financial management and human resources. She wanted to shore up her weaknesses to better handle her new responsibilities.

Robyn's greatest joy as executive director is knowing that she makes a difference. In addition to changing the organization and improving her community, she has also enhanced her employees' professional growth and development.

Robyn found that many of the hard skills she developed before becoming an executive director, such as managing budgets, personnel, and contracts, were extremely useful in her new position. Attending board meetings taught her how to run a meeting. Observing how one executive director interacted with his board, and learning group dynamics, has helped her manage her own board. In addition, soft skills, such as strategic thinking, understanding the difference between governance and management (addressed in **Chapter Four**), relationship-building, and communication, have been extremely helpful. Asking for help (for example, legal counsel) was also important to her success.

> Robyn took advantage of training in finance and human resources.
>
> **observation**

Robyn's greatest challenge is finances. She groans as she remembers the years of budget deficits, trying to keep everyone employed and raising enough funds to make ends meet.

Her other big challenge is human resources. Learning all the laws and regulations is a huge task. But dealing with staff performance is even more

> Revenue generation was a constant concern for Robyn.
>
> **observation**

challenging. She has had to reprimand employees, set up improvement plans, and closely monitor progress. If performance doesn't improve, she lets them go—the most distasteful part of her job.

She overcomes some of these human resources issues by bringing in a consultant, who helps her understand the values, motivations, and communication styles that drive both her and her staff. The consultant also helps her with team-building. Robyn is proud of how her staff has improved its ability to work together and achieve the agency's mission.

Perhaps the hardest part of her job, and the piece she wasn't prepared for, is the unexpected. For example, her previous experience did not prepare her to deal with the real estate issues that come up when liquidating a gift of property or overseeing construction. All of a sudden, she had to learn about selling, buying, zoning, environmental laws, architectural drawings, building loans, hiring general contractors, overseeing construction, inspections, and certificates of occupancy. This is important information they don't teach you in school or in most director-level jobs.

> For Robyn, the hardest part of an executive director's job is dealing with surprises.
>
> **observation**

Robyn wouldn't trade her job for anything. Just as with any job, there are days when she wishes she was doing something else. But most days, she digs into the challenges and celebrates the joys. Robyn knows the difference she is making at all levels—individual, organizational, and community—are well worth her efforts.

Tom's Story

Tom became an executive director by accident. He recognized that a job needed to be done and somebody had to take responsibility. To meet the need, Tom founded an agency. This is no surprise; Tom has always been the type to step up. He responded to an ad in the paper looking for someone to implement supports for people with disabilities coming out of institutions. He has been executive director ever since.

In college, where he studied psychology, Tom worked as a community organizer. As a special education teacher, he developed programs from scratch. As a government staffer, he became a shop steward and union leader. Tom gravitates to leadership positions and has always been a point person for organizational development. He sees what needs to be done and does it.

Tom feels driven to change societal structures and help people. This world view helped him create an organization dedicated to improving lives and changing the community.

Tom started his organization with a $100,000 government grant, the sole source of revenue. His experience as a government social worker came in handy. Tom learned how to navigate a bureaucracy, working within archaic rules, to get things done.

"The first step in learning how to operate within a system is to know all the rules and know them better than anyone else," says Tom. Even today, Tom spends a significant portion of his time poring over governmental legislation and reports so he is ready.

> Tom appreciates the time he spent as a government social worker before becoming executive director of a government-funded agency.
>
> **observation**

As a new executive director, Tom needed help. He took classes in accounting, bookkeeping, administration, evaluation, and supervision. He wanted to shore up his skills in these areas to perform successfully. He also found mentors, whom he met with regularly and who would give him real-life background to complement his academic learning and further develop his skills. By working with mentors, Tom learned about the political systems that governed his agency and how to build relationships within that system.

It wasn't always a smooth road. Tom learned how to be successful through trial and error. "To learn from your successes and failures," Tom says, "you must be brutal with self-evaluation. It is non-negotiable. You must constantly scrutinize yourself and your performance."

"Always do a fidelity check," he says. "Constantly evaluate yourself and others. Be ruthless. And don't be afraid to say what you find. People don't always want to know the truth. But you have to tell it."

Tom underscores the importance of constant evaluation. "You need to acknowledge performance and what works, as well as what doesn't, which can mean making hard decisions. But you have to do this to move forward."

Tom believes the most important characteristic a successful executive director must have is total dedication to the organization's mission. You must constantly keep your eyes on the goal. No matter what happens to distract you, you must always look to your mission.

Changing political players and cuts in government funding are Tom's greatest challenges. "You get to know the systems and the people running those systems and then they're gone in two years. Then you have somebody else running the system that has no understanding of the way things have been. And then you have supervisory people coming in and out who don't know the history or system either. It's why knowing the rules is so important."

Tom believes the most important characteristic a successful executive director must have is total dedication to the organization's mission.

observation

The biggest problem he sees with nonprofits is undercapitalization. In a society where the big fish eat the little ones, Tom recognizes that growth is crucial to survival. An organization needs assets, multiple funding sources, and unrestricted monies. Tom focuses a lot of effort on acquiring assets, diversifying his revenue sources, and building unrestricted funding streams. His objective is to avoid being swallowed up. He wants a sustainable mission.

Tom enjoys the hands-on interaction with the people his organization supports. "I love seeing people succeed on their own." he says.

For Tom, success means forming close relationships, caring for each other; and giving back in some way. He sees these as fundamental to integrating into, and being valued by, the community.

Tom's greatest piece of advice to new executive directors is an old Arabic proverb: *Put your faith in Allah, but tie up your camels.* Believe in your goals, but always have a backup plan. Have faith in your people, but always do fidelity checks.

Tom is driven to change societal structures to better meet its citizens' needs. He is lucky; he gets to do that every day.

> Undercapitalization is a lack of assets.
>
> Assets is the financial term for the value of properties, tangible and intangible, that an organization owns. Assets can include cash, stock, equipment, real estate, receivables, and goodwill.
>
> Unrestricted monies are funds that are not restricted by the donor or funder for any particular program or purpose.
>
> definition

Putting It All Together

The first thing that jumps out about these four executive directors is their absolute passion and unfailing dedication to their organizations' missions. They are fearless in communicating and promoting their missions. They define success in terms of fulfilling the mission. They measure their operations by how they affect people's lives. They connect organizational purpose to real, relatable consequences in the lives of those they serve. Engaging people in the mission is their all-consuming task. No matter what their differences, all of them are, first and foremost, soldiers on a mission.

Mission fulfillment is crucial to agency success. Everything successful executive directors do—every decision they make and program they build—must be driven by their quest to fulfill the mission. Gerry puts it best when he says, "Executive directors need to be proficient managers. Successful executive directors need to also maintain a passion for their organization's mission."

> "Have faith in your people, but always do fidelity checks."
>
> Tom
>
> " "

All four executive directors appreciate the roles their organizations play in the larger community. They see partnerships with other agencies as crucial to their missions, bettering their clients' lives, and improving the community. They see themselves, and their organizations, as part of a greater context: community agencies working together as a cohesive whole. Working with others is an integral part of their jobs.

> "Executive directors need to be proficient managers. Successful executive directors need to also maintain a passion for their organization's mission."
>
> Gerry
>
> " "

Notice, too, their emphasis on generating revenue. Nonprofit organizations must bring in money to fulfill their mission and ensure organizational survival. All four executive directors made some reference to their role in generating revenue. Pat talked about the importance of being familiar with the donor database. Gerry spoke to the value of his grantwriting experience. Robyn talked about her frustration when funds are scarce. Tom underscored his efforts to build assets, diversify revenue streams, and raise unrestricted funds. Clearly, raising money is a top concern for executive directors. Resource development is something every executive director must understand and pursue.

The four executive directors also talked about the importance of mastering information and information channels, such as evaluative financial or outcomes data. Pat talked about the advantage of having donor information at her fingertips. Gerry discussed the impact of knowing your organization's numbers and using them to move the mission forward. Robin spoke to the value of knowing and understanding your agency's financials. Tom emphasized the importance of fidelity checks.

> Executive directors must be proficient in resource development, raising enough money to fulfill their mission and meet their agency's financial obligations.
>
> **observation**

Each of the four acknowledged being only one person and not having all the answers. They all reach out when they need help. They accept their limitations and work to compensate for these weaknesses. Pat found people to help overcome her lack of investment knowledge. Gerry talked about the power of group process. Robyn underscored the importance of getting help on legal matters. And Tom discussed the positive impact of mentorship.

Most of all, every one of these executive directors loves people. They promote people-to-people connections and are driven to improve the well-being of their clients, staff, organizations, and community. They take great joy in growing and developing others and making a difference. Tom enjoys working hands-on with the people he serves. Robin celebrates the satisfaction she experiences working for, with, and through others. Gerry takes great joy in working through people to make things "work right." Pat works to better the plight of the children she serves.

And all of them feel fulfilled. As Pat says, "It is an amazing feeling to be a changing force."

To Recap

- To succeed, executive directors must possess a wide variety of hard and soft skills.
- The most successful executive directors put mission above all else.
- The executive directors must understand their agencies' roles as part of the bigger community.
- Revenue generation is a big part of the job.
- Executive directors must master the evaluative outcomes information available to them.
- Successful executive directors recognize their weaknesses and ask for help when they need it.
- Nonprofit executive directors exhibit a profound love of people.

Chapter Two

I Got the Job! Now What?

IN THIS CHAPTER

- ····➔ Excitement and awe
- ····➔ Celebrating successes
- ····➔ Making unpopular decisions
- ····➔ Developing peer support
- ····➔ Investing in professional development

Excitement and Awe

I was excited. In every previous job, I had always grown my programs. Now, as an executive director, I was looking forward to doing it from a higher level. I knew I was a change agent—I had been one all my professional life. I knew how exciting change could be. And I knew that different people reacted in different ways to change. I was looking forward not only to developing and running a program or department, but to managing an actual organization. What an opportunity to test my skills and see what I was made of. I was excited to see how far I could spread my wings and fly.

But, it was not only my wings that I was testing. I had a staff to lead. I needed to figure out how to let them see how high they could fly, while keeping them on the flight plan.

> A change agent is someone who alters organizational functioning to improve output or acts as a catalyst for change.
>
> definition

I had a board to help me figure out the flight plan—but instead of reporting to an individual, I was now reporting to a group. I had all sorts of personalities and perspectives to manage and was a little scared of having ten bosses to please.

I also had more than a hundred volunteers to manage. After nine years working for a very different executive director, they needed to get to know me and my style.

The organization's success depended on how well I accepted and expressed my leadership. I needed to lead the agency through a transition process: setting a new vision, clearly defining roles, creating a stronger organizational structure while working within the existing one, and building trust that the new structure would work. I didn't know exactly how I was going to accomplish these goals, but I knew that, for the organization to succeed, I had to try.

> A vision is a realistic, credible, attractive future for an organization. A vision statement is an articulation of what you want the organization to be.
>
> definition

Most importantly, I had to bring stability. The past year had not been kind to my agency. After a long-tenured executive director retired that spring, the organization had conducted an extensive executive search and had hired a candidate who did not work out. A part-time, interim executive director was appointed to hold things together. And now they had me. As you might expect, all four executive directors had different ideas about how to run things.

The most damaging part of this leadership upheaval was the devastating financial impact it had on the organization. Donors were not cultivated. Grants were not written. Special event preparations were not made. In short, the relationships the organization needed to succeed financially had shriveled.

I had been brought in to do what I love: create, build, and develop a financially sustainable organization. I was going to do things differently *and* get different results.

So there I was, taking responsibility to rebuild an organization whose survival rested on my leadership. I was both excited and awed.

One thing I learned quickly was that day-to-day decision-making stopped with me. I also learned that I didn't have all the answers. Though I was prepared to make many decisions, there were some for which I was completely unprepared.

Celebrating Success

One of the first things I learned was the absolute importance of celebrating success. I needed it, my staff needed it, my board needed it. When I came on, we were in crisis, and everyone I was leading had been in crisis for a long time. The frontline staff was especially battle scarred. Everyone was anxious about the future and wanted to get off the roller coaster, but no one could articulate what a future off the roller coaster would look like.

Stabilizing the finances was my number one priority. One of the first things I did was create a budget—not only an operating budget but a cash-flow projection. (I talk more about managing finances in **Chapter Six**.) I then took the year's projections and measured our progress monthly. If we met projections, we celebrated, even if the predicted net revenue was negative. At least we knew where we stood and how we were doing. I defined meeting projections as success.

> An operating budget is a written budget for the fiscal year, estimating and itemizing all income by sources and all expenditures by project or department. An operating budget is also called an annual budget or an annual operating budget.
>
> Cash flow is the difference between cash at the beginning of a specific period and the end of that same period. It measures cash coming in and going out.
>
> A stretch budget is a budget based on goals and ideals rather than previous financial performance.
>
> definition

So we would celebrate. I would tell the staff members how important their management had been to the bottom line. I reassured the board that we had achieved what we predicted. In short, I built trust with the people whose efforts could lead to success.

However, we couldn't survive by just improving finances. Mission is what drives an organization. We needed a plan to expand mission, which I did within my first two months. With my board, I put a stretch budget in place so we could bring in the resources we needed to implement our mission. We also evaluated which activities would be crucial to mission success and formulated measurable goals based on our priorities. I worked with my staff to develop action items that supported these goals and attached timelines to them. (For examples of how I set priorities, see **Chapter Five**.)

And then I celebrated every little step that brought us closer to our goals. I wanted the board, staff, and volunteers to see we were moving in the right direction. Not only that, I wanted them to see how their efforts contributed to that forward movement. Teamwork was my goal.

And my efforts paid off. Within six months we had:

- established a call center in another county
- initiated a Save Our Youth campaign
- instituted a texting outreach program for teens
- established an outreach program in two school systems
- trained nineteen new volunteer hotline listeners
- developed a curriculum and trained a core of existing listeners in texting
- become active on several community planning and advisory committees
- developed a relationship with a potential government funder
- held a gala
- implemented a holiday and spring appeal

- analyzed and bid out most of our vendor contracts
- revised all agency job descriptions
- conducted an audit
- developed a board-approved employee manual

By the end of my first year we had also:

- entered into final negotiations to acquire space for a third call center
- developed funding to bring the texting program to four more school systems
- reached out to those school systems
- begun training twenty-seven new volunteer hotline listeners
- instituted a monthly e-newsletter for volunteers, donors, and community partners
- visited with legislators
- hired a volunteer manager
- formed a gala committee and raised forty percent of projected gala revenue a month before the event
- solicited production of professional videos for special events and the website
- submitted eighty-nine foundation and civic funding requests
- cleaned up the donor database
- interviewed foundation program officers and major donors

I couldn't have accomplished all this alone and needed motivated staff, board members, and volunteers to carry out our work. (I talk about working with the board in **Chapter Three** and working with staff and volunteers in **Chapter Eight**).

A strategic plan is a written representation of the organization's strategy to achieve the best fit with its marketplace. A well-written strategic plan articulates organizational vision and converts that vision into measurable objectives and performance targets.

definition

Reaching short-term goals is part of a comprehensive strategic plan. My agency did not have a strategic plan when I got there. Developing one was crucial for long-term success. But for the short term, my quick assessment of the internal and external environments and one-year goals would have to do.

Making Unpopular Decisions

Being at the top is sometimes lonely: All the problems that others can't solve come to the executive director. People rely on the executive director to solve those problems; however, no one can ever solve all problems to everyone's satisfaction. Someone will almost always disagree with a decision the leader made or a process the leader created.

To function as an executive director, I learned quickly that I must be comfortable with negative feedback. I cannot please all the people all the time. To survive professionally, I *must* be able to deal with conflict.

This is especially true for change agents, which I was. An organization in crisis demands change or the organization will not survive. The people in the organization know this and are looking forward to it. However, people also resist change. They feel comfortable with familiar behavior patterns and roles. If you are coming into a crisis, be prepared for these mixed messages. And I have news for you: executive leadership transitions always create organizational crises at one level or another.

As I was preparing to leave my development director job and take on the executive director challenge, my boss put the responsibility of leadership in perspective. "Sh@# always floats to the top," he said. I have never forgotten that. In many ways, the executive director is chief pooper scooper.

Lessons Learned

What came out of that first leadership challenge? In the short term, a lot of discontent. To my staff and volunteers, I was not the warm, caring person my predecessor

My organization was in leadership and financial crisis when I took over. Analyzing budget information a month before I started, it became clear that we couldn't sustain the operating budget. Cutting the dues, travel, and staff development lines was easy. However, that was not enough. Since personnel was our biggest expense, we needed to look long and hard at staffing. My first act as executive director was to cut my office manager's hours. Three months later, I laid someone off. Not pleasant experiences or popular decisions.

What did I do right? I discussed the issues and made the decisions with my board's full support. Making personnel cuts was not easy for them, either. But the board had to make sure our mission carried forward. They needed me to make the hard decisions and carry them through.

To get through it, I sought out support from another executive director who had experienced layoffs, took time to get together with friends, and maintained some semblance of balance with people who knew and liked me. (I talk about the importance of developing peer support in the next section. I talk about work/life balance in **Chapter Twelve.**)

stories from the real world

had been. To some, I did not understand how crucial staff was to agency operations; I made rash decisions without taking their needs into account; and I didn't listen. There had not been time to develop a trusting relationship. My actions, to them brutal and devastating, were the only things they really knew about me.

The timing was unfortunate. But my actions, in the long term, strengthened the agency. Not only did the organization survive financially, we were later able to restructure and build staff.

It was not easy when there were only two of us left in the office. We experienced overwhelming workloads, but these lean operations allowed us to prioritize our responsibilities. We analyzed tasks in light of our individual skill sets, and divided them based on our strengths. We were more productive, more satisfied and started to gel as a team.

When the agency stabilized financially, my director and I could analyze what wasn't getting done and develop a new job description based on organizational needs, as well as team strengths and weaknesses. This made interviewing and choosing the right candidate much easier. Now, we have three staff who work together as a cohesive team.

Another good thing to come out of this strengths-based team approach was the way we used interns. Just as we had for our volunteer manager, we developed optimal job descriptions for our program interns. The interns functioned effectively within well-articulated job expectations, provided the organization great value at no cost, and gained real-world job experience. Plus, we enhanced the organization's reputation among new people who would spread the word about our work.

The most gratifying response to the staffing crisis came from our volunteers—the most dedicated group of people I have ever met. They stepped up to the plate, took stock of their own needs, outlined tasks that had to be done, and took initiative, reaching out to less active volunteers. It was a sight to behold—volunteers reaching out to volunteers, something every development director and volunteer manager dreams of.

Making tough, unpopular decisions is not easy, and there are negative repercussions. But managed correctly, the long-term results can be positive.

> I was humbled by my volunteers' responses. I cannot say enough about them. Even though, as an executive director, I am not involved in their day-to-day work, I make it a priority to let them know how valuable they are to me and the organization.
>
> **stories from the real world**

Developing Peer Support

One thing I did right was establish peer support systems before I even started. I began my quest for support during the job search. I interviewed a long-time executive director and asked him loads of questions about the hard and soft skills I needed for the position, as well as his struggles, successes, and challenges. When I was offered the job, I asked my current boss to list the three most important priorities he saw as an executive director. I also used the CharityChannel network to ask the same question. The answers I got helped me tremendously. While

Who can you talk to?

food for thought

they didn't necessarily solve all my problems, they gave me a framework to handle the more perplexing ones.

Executive directors are very busy people. Often, support meant a ten-minute phone conversation, if that. Getting together with another executive director was challenging. First, each of us had hectic schedules running our own organizations. Second, we faced emergencies and had to cancel appointments. Third, we struggled finding enough time for our own families, much less each other.

I was lucky. I developed a peer support system with two executive directors. I needed all the support they gave me. Even better, they had been in their positions for at least twenty-five years. When I faced a new situation, they had already encountered it. They analyzed my problems and gave concrete solutions. Because I often received two perspectives, I got a well-rounded view. They provided insights into my organizational issues that might never have occurred to me.

I maintained relationships with two executive directors whom I trusted and with whom I could be open and frank. When you find peers you can trust and count on for good counsel, latch onto them. Such friends are worth their weight in gold.

stories from the real world

I was fortunate to have these two executive directors in my corner, not only for their sage wisdom, but also because they took time for me. They both managed bigger agencies than mine. One even had to make dinner appointments with his wife to see her on a regular basis. Yet, they both took time to listen to me and help me through some perplexing issues. These seasoned executive directors gave me something I could not give back—experience and wisdom, things I desperately needed.

In addition to advice, I needed their support. I needed to not feel alone and know that my challenges were manageable. Other people had faced the same issues and had come out intact. Talking to my peers helped calm me when I felt overwhelmed and gave me hope for a better future. The trusting relationships I developed with other executive directors have been invaluable.

Investing in Professional Development

Another thing I did right was invest in an executive coach. My transition to the executive office was significant. When I accepted the position, I moved into a new organizational role. Previously, I had been an employee under the guidance of a single supervisor. Organizational goals and vision were defined for me. In this new role, I reported to a ten-person board. I had to define the organizational vision and goals with my board and infuse it to my staff and volunteers. Before, the buck stopped with someone else. Now it stopped with me. The organizational culture was defined by someone else. Now, it depended on my own personal values and worldview. Before, my actions directly affected only one department. Now, my actions affected everyone in the organization. I needed to come to terms with executive leadership *fast.*

> No one understands what it's like to be an executive director except another executive director. No matter how close my relationships with my board and staff, they just didn't know what I was facing in quite the same way as my peers. I was lucky to have such open, trusting relationships with two peers. I believe that every new executive director should seek out this type of support.
>
> **Lessons Learned**

Another transition was going from a large, financially stable agency with firmly established leadership to a small one experiencing a financial and leadership crisis. In the past, with a $30 million budget, coming in $10,000 or $20,000 under goal had no significant impact on the agency. Now, with a $260,000 budget, $10,000 could mean success or failure. In my previous role, it was easy to demonstrate organizational credibility: the agency had years of program growth; the financials had been good for years; and, with six hundred employees, it had a comprehensive infrastructure. In the new agency, I didn't have these advantages. A small organization, with four staff, including me, did not need an elaborate

> Changing jobs is one of the top stressors any American faces. According to Dr. Julius Segal, events that generate loss, leave you feeling helpless, or have lasting consequences cause major stress. Career transitions fall into all of these categories.
>
> **observation**

infrastructure. Management systems were more informal than with my past employer. This informality, and the series of leadership transitions, gave our external constituencies, funders, and community partners' doubts about our credibility.

Then there were the changes to my day-to-day schedule. As executive director, I have broader responsibilities. My days and weeks are jam-packed, and I have more issues to deal with more often. Emergencies throw a wrench into my best laid plans. I went from making all of my appointments on time to sometimes showing up late or canceling at the last minute. As development director, I worked evenings maybe once a week. Now, I'm often out at least two evenings a week and two Saturdays a month. Gone are the days when I took solid, two-week vacations.

Becoming an executive director was a major transition for me. There were many adjustments in a short period. Friend and peer support helped, but I needed someone to help me think through my goals and challenges, develop my own solutions, and hold me accountable for maintaining work/life balance. So, I hired an executive coach. (I talk more about work/life balance in **Chapter Twelve**.)

My executive coach helped me handle my transitions. I had someone objective to talk to who was not personally involved in my organization. I value that perspective. She helped me think through my goals, look at my challenges more objectively, solve problems, and consider the consequences of my actions. While leaving the decision up to me, she helped me better understand my work and communication styles and how they contributed to my

> An executive coach is a certified professional who helps leaders reach their fullest potential. An executive coach builds on the core drivers and fundamental philosophies that motivate their clients, helping them become strong leaders, creative and strategic thinkers, and influential business people.
>
> A coach is not a therapist. Unlike a therapist or counselor, who deals with issues from the past, an executive coach deals with the here and now. A therapist helps you understand yourself in light of your personal history. An executive coach helps you understand the skills and abilities you have (or need) to succeed in the workplace.
>
> definition

strengths and weaknesses. She also helped me understand the people I work with and how to approach them. Although I was pretty self-aware before I hired her, my executive coach helped me learn how to function in my new role—invaluable insights to have during any transition.

For example, working with a board was new to me. (I talk more about working with the board in **Chapter Four**.) I had to get used to different personalities and styles. I would talk to my coach about my exasperation dealing with certain strong personalities, and my fears that I would never meet a goal with them. My coach let me talk about my fears and frustrations, helped me see how I perceived their leadership and communication styles, and showed me that my interpretations were not always what they were trying to communicate. She also helped me see how my leadership and communications style came across to them.

What an eye-opener to have someone let me talk about my frustrations and propose my own solutions, but then point out how those solutions might be perceived. She helped me clarify the problems, as I saw them, think through the consequences of my solutions, and left the decisions up to me. Sometimes, the consequences were what I wanted. Other times, they were not and I changed my behaviors. Occasionally, I needed to accept unsatisfactory results to move forward. My coach was an excellent investment, well worth the price, which I paid personally.

I took many actions to move into my new role. I defined and celebrated success, created a short-term plan, with input from board and staff, and developed a professional support system. There were many things I needed to learn. I am grateful to my board, staff, volunteers, and network for helping me succeed.

To Recap

- The transition to executive director is significant.
- Define and celebrate success with board, staff, and volunteers.
- Learn to deal with negative feedback.
- Create short-term objectives.
- Build up your peer support.
- If you can, invest in an executive coach.

Chapter Three

Me Getting to Know Them—Them Getting to Know Me

IN THIS CHAPTER

- In the beginning
- The honeymoon period
- When the honeymoon is over
- The continuing relationship

In the Beginning

About a month before I started, I was introduced to the agency and community as the new executive director. It was a heady experience. The board president sent the email announcement to staff and volunteers. The press release was picked up by local media. I was introduced at an organizational town hall. All these interactions were positive. And so began the relationship with my new organization.

After the board president's announcement to staff and volunteers, I sent my own emails. I wanted them to know who I was, in my own words, and start building a relationship with them.

In sending out these communiqués, I realized that each constituency required a different approach. Instead of just meeting my donors'/co-workers'/supervisor's needs and expectations, I needed to please a much larger and more diverse group. I still had to satisfy my donors, but instead of a supervisor, I now reported to a board of directors. Instead of co-workers, I had colleagues from other nonprofits. I had a large paid and unpaid staff, and my roles were different with each constituency.

> The board of directors is the body with legal and fiduciary responsibility to carry out a nonprofit's mission. A nonprofit agency's board is ultimately responsible to the public. The board is also commonly referred to as a board of trustees.
>
> definition

My board needed to hear about my preliminary vision, group facilitation, and leadership skills. My staff was more concerned about my leadership style, priorities, and expectations. My volunteers had to believe I recognized the importance of their work and how valuable they are to the mission.

I remember crafting those first emails and trying to put myself in their shoes. I wanted to connect with them, to communicate a part of myself, so they would understand exactly where I was coming from. I wanted everyone in the organization to know I was aware of their issues and eager to address them. I had to communicate that I understood their roles, valued each of them, and recognized what they contributed.

Unfortunately, the transition from the last executive director had been tough. His replacement did not work out and there was a lag before I arrived. In one year, there had been four different people in the role. I wanted everyone to know I was confident in my abilities to resolve this crisis and was there to stay. In other words, I was ready and willing to enter into a committed relationship with them.

> Being an organization's executive director is much like being married. However, instead of two individuals committing to one another, it is one individual and a whole organization making that commitment.
>
> food for thought

The Honeymoon

Research shows that just like newly married couples, every new executive director enjoys a honeymoon, particularly with the board. A honeymoon is a period of unusual harmony following the establishment of a new relationship. The board spent significant effort finding the right candidate. They were relieved that the grueling search was over and looked forward to welcoming a new leader. They were excited that their hopes and dreams would be fulfilled.

For me, the honeymoon lasted about six months, during which I enjoyed tremendous latitude. The board was excited about my skills and was looking forward to positive change. The board loved that I made firm decisions and stuck to them. Since there was no way to measure my performance, other than my past accomplishments, the board readily accepted the goals I set and believed in my ability to meet them. The board supported me unconditionally.

I began the job in October, just as the budget process was beginning. One of my first tasks was budget forecasting. Because of all the previous transitions, finances were not good, and we were not meeting budget projections.

My background is in fundraising. As a development director, I was very successful at generating revenue and accustomed to developing stretch budgets. After all, if you don't set high goals, you aren't going to achieve your potential. My solution was to develop an organizational stretch budget, in which we would be okay if we only met a percentage of the goal. I thought I knew what I was doing.

By presenting a stretch budget, I set myself up for failure. When I created the budget, I had made some incorrect assumptions. Several board members tried to warn me that a more realistic budget would be more appropriate, but I wanted to prove myself. The board wanted to support me unconditionally, so it went along with my decision.

Four months later, I had to significantly revise the budget based on a worst case scenario—both revenues and cost projections. That way, the board knew exactly what we needed to meet minimum goals. I didn't look as good and learned a big lesson.

Lessons Learned

I was also enamored. This agency had been through a lot of trauma. I was impressed by the board, staff, volunteers, donors, and community partners. Despite the protracted leadership and financial problems, many people had stuck with them.

I was also impressed by the sense of mission throughout the organization. I had worked in nonprofits for almost twenty years and had never seen such a deep commitment to mission. Whatever crises we were facing, I knew this dedication to mission would carry us through. I am forever indebted to my predecessors for creating a pervasive mission-driven culture.

> Many people have a difficult relationship with power. One way I dealt with this dynamic was to acknowledge my newly acquired authority. To lead effectively, I had to be aware of the power I had and think through how best to use it.
>
> **Lessons Learned**

I also loved being part of multiple teams: board, staff, and volunteers. I believe the best thinking comes through teamwork. I enjoyed the different roles I played in each group and the respect afforded me by everyone in the organization.

I learned the hopes and dreams of my staff, board, and volunteers and shared my hopes and dreams with them. Within the first month, I met individually with every board member, getting their perspectives on our strengths, weaknesses, and challenges. I talked to the staff members about their expectations for me, what was working for them, and what was not. I kept building relationships, and began developing a culture of teamwork. I let everyone know they were a vital part of the solution.

I also defined roles and responsibilities, especially for the staff and volunteers. I worked with the board on setting goals and priorities. I instituted a monthly newsletter, in which I shared my vision with all constituencies. I started laying the foundation for future growth while my ideas were still accepted and supported.

And it worked. The foundation that I laid in the beginning served me well after the honeymoon was over.

When the Honeymoon Is Over

Every honeymoon ends, it's the natural course of things. In a marriage, you and your spouse get to know each and become comfortable. The same was true with me and my organization. Over time, my staff and board came to understand that I was there to stay. I also developed a track record—some of my goals had been met while some had not. Over time, my solid partnership made it safe for both parties to express disagreement.

Although it doesn't feel like it, the end of the honeymoon is a good sign. It means the relationship has grown strong enough to handle some tension. As my honeymoon ended, people felt their relationship with me was solid enough to take risks. Others trusted me to accept them, even when their opinions differed from mine. People could bring their uniqueness to the team.

I missed the unconditional freedom, but there is more strength when people bring their whole selves to the table, rather than just going along with everything I say. As an individual who was new to the organization, I did not know all the answers or all the facts. I did not even know all the questions to ask. As a result, I needed help from others—their perspectives and questions.

> The honeymoon's duration varies, depending on the situation. Rest assured, you will know when it ends. The best way to prepare is to anticipate. Honeymoons always end. Every marriage goes through it; every organization with a new executive director goes through it as well.
>
> practical tip

I embraced the tension. I knew that true teamwork was finally possible and that I could accomplish more through my team than as an individual. I deepened my relationships with board, staff, and volunteers, developing an intimacy that is extremely fulfilling and only executive directors can experience. I could now fully develop my leadership skills and reach my potential. The end of the honeymoon is an exciting place to be, full of potential, possibility, and growth.

How I responded to the conflict that arose when people showed their independence laid the foundation for the rest of the year, and quite possibly, the rest of my tenure.

My research into organizational behavior and development has been crucial to helping me understand organizational dynamics. In addition, my studies in social psychology and sociology have helped me understand group behavior and process. If you are going to lead an organization, I highly recommend investigating these fields.

practical tip

The Continuing Relationship

Consistency. Honesty. Forthrightness. Integrity.

These are the values on which I base my leadership; values I developed long before I became an executive director. I knew what kind of leader I wanted to be and the boundaries I wanted to create. (I talk more about how personal values affect corporate culture in **Chapter Eleven**.)

Executive transition is tough on an agency. At one level, people understand why their previous executive left and wish them the best. But they also feel abandoned, particularly if the executive director left for another opportunity. There is always fear of the unknown: how will we survive without the former exec's strengths and institutional IQ? What will the new person be like? How will things change? Will we be better or worse off? These concerns are common during leadership changes. It's up to you to help them feel better. (I talk about working with the board in **Chapter Four** and working with staff and volunteers in **Chapter Eight**.)

I first had to deal with those unspoken feelings of abandonment, which some people experience more strongly than others. In my case, having replaced a permanent executive director who resigned within a month, the abandonment issue was especially acute. It was particularly hard for the board members, who had invested so much time and energy searching for the new leader. The only way I could deal with their feelings was to hear them out. They needed to process. My role was not to fix it for them but to make it safe for them to express themselves.

As an executive director, know your values and boundaries. They will be tested.

Lessons Learned

I also needed to show, through my actions, that I was not going to leave. It was a good four months before my board stopped joking about my impending resignation, but I was there to stay. Time and my consistent presence were the only things that could prove that.

I also had to address fear of the unknown. Fear is a powerful motivating emotion and, like feelings of abandonment, will probably be unspoken. By articulating who I was, what I stood for, and what I was there to do, I slowly put these fears to rest. Granted, I couldn't do that in day one—I hadn't had time to completely grasp the organization and its issues. But I could start doing it after about six weeks.

I don't have control over my environment or a crystal ball to predict the future. However, I can deal with reality as it is today, be open and forthright about the issues we face, put a plan in place, and be brutally honest.

Brutal honesty is not always popular or easy. Some people don't want to hear the truth; they don't want their perception of reality rocked. Some don't want to acknowledge the truth because they don't want to see how they contributed to that reality.

> Having worked in development for so long, I knew what kind of information funders wanted about an organization's executive leadership. I worked with my public relations person to write my one-page profile. I then shared it with my board and staff and put it on our website. That piece helped establish my credibility, as well as the organization's, and was a great vehicle to help people get to know me.
>
> **Lessons Learned**

However, if you are not honest, people will not trust you. It may take a while, but eventually the truth will be revealed. If your perceptions of reality reflect what others see, you will be trusted. If they don't, you will not. If you are manipulating circumstances to shade reality, proceed at your own detriment. If no one trusts you, no one will follow you, in which case you will not be a leader. No matter how tempting it is to shade reality, don't give in.

Brutal honesty does not mean telling everybody everything. Honesty means telling the truth, not revealing confidential information. There is a fine line between being honest and being prudent in your disclosures.

Some decisions should not be shared. Human resources and personnel decisions are, by nature, confidential. When I had to eliminate a position, I wanted the person being laid off to be the first person to know. It was not a decision I could share with other staff or volunteers.

stories from the real world

Every executive director needs to define how close to the vest they want to play it. There is no magic line.

The key to establishing long-term trusting relationships is consistency. Consistent words and actions generate trust. I must also make sure my words reflect reality, and not some idealized version of reality.

I say what I do and do what I say. I am reliable and dependable. I don't cover up the truth. I am upfront and forthright—you always know where you stand with me. I prize integrity. Those characteristics, I believe, are what made me a good fundraiser and have helped me succeed as an executive director.

In the beginning, things are good. And then things change. Be prepared for the honeymoon to end. Embrace the tensions and joys that come with deepening relationships. Help the organization deal with abandonment and fear. Know your values and abide by them. Let people know you. Be honest. Be consistent. Develop trust.

To Recap

- Start building relationships with board, staff, and volunteers before the job starts.
- Use the honeymoon to lay the foundation for your tenure.
- When the honeymoon ends, embrace the gift of tension.
- For successful long-term relationships, know your values, be consistent, and be honest.

Chapter Four

Working with the Board

IN THIS CHAPTER

- Defining roles and expectations
- The relationship with the board president
- Dealing with group dynamics

When I first got the new job, I asked my old boss to list an executive director's top three priorities. "That's easy," he said. "The board, the board, and the staff." I asked the same question to the CharityChannel network, who confirmed the importance of managing board relations. Once I started the job and began networking with other executive directors, board relations and board development were chief concerns. Obviously, working with the board was going to be critically important. (I talk about working with the staff in **Chapter Eight**.)

As a first-time executive director, with a one-year tenure under my belt, I am not professing to know even a fraction of what it takes to build and sustain strong, long-term board relationships. But I do know what the transition from development director to executive director was like.

Defining Roles and Expectations

As best practices support, clearly defined roles and responsibilities, for both the executive director and the board, help everyone know what is expected of them and who is responsible for what. Defined expectations help the relationship between board and executive director run smoothly.

Board Recruitment

Hopefully, your board has a document outlining board service expectations and individual responsibilities. In my organization, this instrument has been extremely valuable in recruiting and orienting board members to their roles.

Part of my job is to help identify and recruit board members. In my organization this is not me bringing in whomever I want for the board to vote on. I am *not* the board. I do not have complete control, nor do I want it. We function as a governance team, jointly setting vision and monitoring progress. Both the board members and I felt it was important that they maintain their independence and freely provide their unique perspectives. I needed that kind of input. The board had to play an active role in recruitment.

Identifying and recruiting board members was a group process. My first board retreat came three months after I started. We had just lost two members and were looking for replacements, so we took the opportunity to analyze what we all brought to the table. We determined group strengths and weaknesses, then outlined what we would look for in new board members.

This was an extremely helpful exercise. We detailed what we could, and could not, do well, which made us keenly aware of our group biases and decision-making blind spots. We agreed on the type of person we wanted to fill our ranks. In other words, we gelled as a team.

> In our search for new board members, we approached, and were approached by, potential recruits. With written guidelines and a thorough understanding of who we were looking for, the board and I coordinated recruitment. We were all working from the same playbook.
>
> This mutual understanding helped potential board members understand their roles. It also helped new recruits feel confident in agency leadership, as they saw us working together towards the same goals.
>
> In the end, we built a stronger governance team.
>
> **Lessons Learned**

Agency Governance

The board has ultimate responsibility for organizational governance—not the executive director. It has the legal and en though my board understands, intellectually, that I am different from y predecessor, it takes time to internalize these differences and expect fferent behaviors. This was particularly difficult for board members who ly experienced my predecessor's leadership style. Instinctively, they rely their past experiences for guidance.

is is not a bad thing, it is simply the reality. People need new experiences adjust expectations, and new experiences are a function of time.

had to counter the "it's never been done that way before" syndrome. I stened to my board, asked what had gone right and wrong, reinforced my alues, strengths, and experiences, and explained how I would use them tackle our issues. I let the board process new information with me, and stened to feedback, both positive and negative, on my plans. In short, I nticipated push back and let the board process the past as I paved the oad for the future. More importantly, I listened to the board and created a mutually collaborative relationship rather than a competitive, contentious one.

Of course, it wasn't easy. Although I was experienced at creating a vision and fulfilling goals, I was new to managing fears. It was easy for me to focus on the future. However, I had to learn how to manage other people's fear of failure. For me, failure is an opportunity to learn. For the board, failure meant we didn't stay in business. Most of my board members felt that more acutely than I did. They were war-weary and tired of going from crisis to crisis. In many ways, they saw me as their last hope.

I really didn't understand this sense of desperation for a long time. I'm not sure I ever did. My brusque, forthright, and brutally

My predecessor and I are *very* different people. For example, I am a strong planner and don't like dealing with last minute emergencies. By contrast, my predecessor was not a good planner but excelled at dealing with sudden crises. Both approaches have pluses and minuses.

It took a while for the board to adjust to my style. The board/ executive director relationship had to be redesigned to accommodate my strengths and weaknesses. Our relationship s very different from anything they experienced under my predecessor.

stories from the real world

fiduciary duty to ensure the mission is carried forward and finances managed wisely. If there is a lawsuit against the organization, board are on the suit, along with the executive director.

The executive director works at the behest of the board. The executiv director is hired, evaluated and, if need be, fired by the board. The executive director implements the vision and abides by the policies t board sets. While the board delegates organizational operations, it is ultimately responsible for agency governance.

Understanding this relationship was critically important for me. As executive director, I do not control the board—I work with it as an ex member. As the board memb changes with time, I will have influence, being the most stab board presence, as well as hav the greatest familiarity with th agency's day-to-day operation But I, as the executive director, not the final decision maker, th board is.

> Governance is the action, manner, or system of making policy and ensuring adherence.
>
> definition

One challenge is mastering many different roles I play: the boss as chi executive officer; team player as ex officio board member; and staff subordinate as board employee. It's a challenging juggling act for both executive director and the board.

Defining the Board/Executive Director Relationship

Every executive director needs to create their own board/executive director relationship. For some reason, I wasn't expecting to work so hard to define ours.

> Ex officio means holding a position or membership due t the power or influence of one office or position, rather than by election or appointment. E officio board members may h voting rights, depending on t organization's by-laws.
>
> definition

Unless you are the founder, you will be following a previous leader, who had a different personality, strengths, and weaknesses. This person might even have had different values.

honest style didn't calm their fears, especially when I expressed frustration at the problems I found. If I had it to do again, I would still be honest, but I'm not sure I would express my emotions so strongly. I don't believe it helped.

On the other hand, I'm glad I was upfront about the issues I found and how I was dealing with them. Though I may not have brought calm, I did let the board know who I was. Because I was so transparent, the board learned to trust me. And because I was so upfront, the board members knew where I needed help. In addition to being new to the organization, the board and the executive director role, I was dealing with some difficult circumstances. Ultimately, by being upfront to my board, I gained more than I lost.

Developing the board/executive relationship was not all one-sided. We built this wonderful, collaborative relationship *together*. I brought attributes to the table, as did my board members. For example, as I was forthright with them, they were also forthright with me. Both sides worked towards a collaborative relationship. They accepted me, with all my inexperience and shortcomings, worked with me and helped when I asked. It wasn't just me handling the board—it was also the board handling me.

Governance Versus Management

> Before you take on the executive director role, know your style's pros and cons.
>
> practical tip

Boards and executive directors often clash over board oversight. Both sides struggle to define where governance ends and management begins, as shown by the many materials on board governance and development. I was not prepared for the oversight role's ambiguity. Fortunately, I wasn't the only one who thought the issue needed to be addressed.

The board governs and the executive director manages. As the governing body, the board is responsible for setting the vision; hiring an executive director to implement that vision; setting boundaries on how the executive director fulfills the vision; and measuring progress. The board also imposes rules to govern how it operates and manages itself. As chief executive officer, the executive director manages the agency's operations to fulfill the board's vision, abiding by the board's expressed limitations.

> I am lucky to have such a great relationship with my board. Other executive directors have told me that, over time, they have had both collaborative and contentious boards. No doubt, one day I will also have challenging board relations. For now, I am thankful that board relations are good.
>
> stories from the real world

The complications come from the executive director's overlapping roles as ex officio board member and staff subordinate board employee. I'm not sure this tension is ever resolved; at least it wasn't in my first year. The boundaries between the two roles are fluid, and each board member approaches the relationship differently.

It's crucial to have documents outlining roles and responsibilities. We used the board responsibilities document to streamline board recruitment. When I was contacted, I could speak intelligently about board service requirements per board instructions. Also, when we met potential board members, we had a detailed description to share.

The document was not something the board made up and put on a shelf, it's a living, breathing document used to monitor its own performance. I had very little to do with its revisions, except to review and comment on them as they affected agency operations.

> Whereas governance is the process of making and enforcing policy, management is the responsibility for, and control of, an organization. In other words, it is the administration of a business or company.
>
> definition

I have much more control over documents that govern my own yearly objectives, building staff action plans to meet those objectives, creating budgets and forecasts, making personnel decisions, and assisting with the strategic plan.

Staff action plans and personnel decisions are my domain. At first, I had to negotiate this with the board, but it was important that my staff have one supervisor, as opposed to several board members approaching them directly. I didn't want any mixed messages and confusion from multiple inputs. So, hiring, evaluating, firing, and developing staff is my role.

Evaluating my work is the board's role. It agreed to measure my performance based on how well I reach my annual objectives. Because these objectives cascade down to staff action plans, evaluating my performance encompasses all parts of the organization and is a reflection on my managerial skills.

> It is *not* my place to run the board—it is the board president's place to do that.
>
> **food for thought**

The board and I created the vision together. I drafted my goals and objectives based on board priorities. Together, we reviewed my draft and made revisions. We did not have a strategic plan when I took the job. One of the big tasks the board started during my first year was defining their vision and creating a strategic plan to meet that vision. A lot of people had input into that effort.

Budgets and forecasts are my responsibility to create and implement and the board's to approve and monitor. The board has a legal and fiduciary responsibility to maintain financial oversight. With dual budget oversight,

> The board decided to evaluate me in six month increments, according to our fiscal year. Within my first six weeks, we developed a strategic dashboard outlining the next year's objectives. Six months into the year, I updated the chart to show my progress and sent it to the board president, who distributed it to the whole board for comment. The president and another board member compiled the comments and sat down with me to go over them.
>
> I sweated that first evaluation, not knowing what to expect. However, we had to revise the process. I needed to be more specific on defining benchmarks for each six-month period. Board members also needed more direction on the specificity of their comments.
>
> Overall, the comments were good. People thought I had done a great job, considering the circumstances. I found it very helpful when comments were specific—pointing out both my strengths and weaknesses—constructive, and focused on attaining future goals.
>
> **stories from the real world**

finances became everyone's responsibility, especially revenue generation. Some board members took on traditional fundraising roles and all contributed to improving the bottom line. (I talk more about resource development in **Chapter Seven**.)

Being aware of my own limitations, I asked for specific policies that outlined what I *couldn't* do. My reasoning was that there are a thousand ways to skin a cat. Rather than articulating all the ways I can accomplish an objective, a never-ending list, tell me what I can't do. Because it is more contained, the "can't list" is a more manageable, simpler guide to evaluating executive actions. At the same time, listing only the limitations gave me latitude to solve everyday problems. In the end, my behavior was appropriately evaluated and the board was free to focus on real governance issues, like board roles and strategic planning, instead of how much I spent on office supplies.

> Money issues are the toughest to deal with and can generate vexing power struggles.
>
> **Lessons Learned**

I was very happy when the board articulated its roles and responsibilities and developed a strategic plan. For a long time, it had been in a day-to-day, crisis management mode. I had been there less than a year when it started focusing on governance. I was doing my job, freeing up the board to do its job. In turn, I would get the strategic guidance I needed, a win-win.

Relationship with the Board President

The most crucial board relationship is with the president. I have relied heavily on the president, particularly in my first few months at the agency. During that time, I was in constant contact with her, often two to three times a day. This was necessary because the organization was in a leadership and financial crisis, and I was brand new. I still don't know whether my heavy reliance on the board president was a good or bad thing, but it did create a robust, supportive relationship that continues to this day.

Because there was so much communication, the board president and I got to know each other very well, very quickly. We also got used to working together. I needed her to give me organizational background, so I could understand why we were in crisis. I also needed insights into how problems had been resolved in the past, as well as where the organization had been, so I could chart a plausible course forward. The board president was invaluable in giving me this background.

The president was also crucial in making sure my voice was heard by the board. As an ex officio member, I do not run or control the board, the president does. Just as I wanted one voice to communicate with my staff, I also wanted one voice from the board. That was part of the president's role. My president did not make board decisions with me but rather let me know what information the board needed to make those decisions. She also gave insights into how to present information so the board would understand the agency's situation. I have needed her insight to function effectively.

Our relationship is based on a deep, mutual respect. We do not try to change each other, but rather see equals with valid viewpoints—a team, working for the organization and the community. We appreciate our differences, acknowledge the strengths each of us bring to the table, recognize our limitations and have developed a trust so strong we can be vulnerable with each other.

I don't know if this is a normal relationship between an executive director and board president, but I am glad I have it. Even better, my relationship with the president has trickled down to the entire board.

Dealing with Group Dynamics

One of my big changes in the new role was reporting to a group, as opposed to an individual. Working with a board was a new experience for me. On the plus side, I had no preconceived notions about the relationship. However, I also had no idea what I wanted from the relationship. I didn't know how to deal with the board, what I wanted from it, what was possible, and what wasn't. The good news is that, with help, it didn't take long to figure it out.

> The quality of the board/executive director relationship can determine a nonprofit's success or failure. The board president/executive director relationship plays a critical role in this equation.
>
> **observation**

A good marriage takes a lot of work, requiring complete acceptance, unfailing dedication and loyalty, common goals, solid

A major reason for my good relationship with the board is the board president's excellent group process and communication skills. Without her, I would not be as successful.

Lessons Learned

communication, and a good sense of humor. Marriage between two people is difficult enough. Marriage between a person and a group of ten is a real challenge.

In working with a board, instead of dealing with one person's perspective, personality, and personal history, you are dealing with ten, twenty, thirty, or more. Factor in the group perspective, personality, and history —and a fluid definition of executive director's role —and you can have a real mess. Managing group dynamics is one of the most challenging and rewarding things I do as executive director and equally challenging for the board president.

Group dynamics is one of the challenges my executive coach helped me navigate. In addition to helping me understand my work style, my coach helped me appreciate my board members' approaches. She taught me how different personality types express themselves, which helped me remain objective when our styles differed. She also helped me understand how to find common ground with people who communicated differently, crucial to building support. Do I have this aspect of my job down completely? No, I am still learning how to work with a very diverse group as one entity.

One reality I had to accept was, sometimes, 67 percent means success. Not everyone agrees with everyone else all the time. Some people are more committed to specific courses than others. Sometimes, decisions could be tabled until later. If decisions couldn't wait, we had to agree that 67 percent was good enough. I don't like it when people are displeased and prefer a complete consensus to 67 percent. But sometimes consensus is just not possible and a decision has to be made. That was a difficult adjustment.

Group dynamics are the processes and emotions that determine interactions in social groups.

definition

Sometimes people are passionate about an issue and express very strong opinions. I could have taken some of those opinions personally, interpreting them as a slight on my abilities. Occasionally I did, but not often. I came into the job knowing that what people expressed said more about them and their issues than it did about me and my performance. Some people call this having a thick skin. Believe me, as an executive director, you need one.

> The first thing my executive coach did was have me complete a DISC (Dominance, Inducement, Submission, Compliance) assessment, which helped me analyze my natural work style. As time went on, she also helped me understand how to work with other styles. This analysis taught me to appreciate how others communicate and how to approach them, even if their style grated on me.
>
> **stories from the real world**

For example, my board was weary and wanted off the roller coaster. Sometimes, board members would express dissatisfaction that finances had not improved enough. I could have taken their misgivings personally and gotten defensive. Rather than addressing the need to generate adequate resources, I would have been addressing my job performance and reinforcing that fundraising is only an executive director's responsibility. My relationship with the board would have deteriorated.

The underlying problem was not my job performance, it was the finances, specifically revenue generation (I discuss revenue generation in **Chapter Seven**). Building organizational relationships is both an executive director and a board function. So when the "frustrations over finances" conversation came up, it revealed more about the board than it did about me. Rather than getting defensive about my performance, I addressed our financial issues from a collaborative, relationship-building perspective. This approach led to productive solutions and preserved our relationship. The board was

> Accepting help was especially important to overcome my weaknesses. Rather than see offers of help as slights on my competence, I acknowledged my weaknesses and accepted those offers. The board was not there to find fault with me, it wanted the strongest possible organization.
>
> **Lessons Learned**

not there to point out my faults and complain, it was there to help the organization continue its good work. Financial solvency was part of that picture.

I have such a rosy attitude because the relationship with my board is so good. If there had been severe conflicts, I probably would have trouble interpreting their actions so positively.

Dealing with the board is a top priority for an executive director. One of the biggest predictors of organizational success is the board/executive director relationship. Understand your role and the board's. Develop a good working relationship with your board president. Understand the complexity of group dynamics and deal with them. Know that the topics boards bring up say more about it than you.

To Recap

- Develop a mutual understanding of board roles, responsibilities, and gaps.
- Define your own relationship with the board.
- Understand board governance roles.
- Understand your management responsibilities and how they fit in with board governance roles.
- Develop a good working relationship with your board president.
- Understand and manage group dynamics.

Chapter Five

When Everything Demands Your Attention

IN THIS CHAPTER

- Structuring workload
- Prioritizing tasks
- Delegating to others

One thing that took me by surprise was the enormity of the position. All of a sudden, I was responsible for human resources, information technology, communications, marketing, revenue generation, cost containment, cash flow, volunteer management, policy setting and enforcement, and board relations—all of it, all at once, every day. I was swamped.

In this chapter, I discuss what I did to get through my first year. (I talk more in depth about building for the future in **Chapter Ten**.)

Structuring Workload

I learned that an executive director must accomplish a lot of daily tasks, while also dealing with unforeseen emergencies. No matter how well I plan my week, something urgent always crops up. The job can be frenetic. As an executive director, I must:

- Manage operations
- Satisfy funders and donors

- Inform and inspire board, staff, and volunteers
- Listen to clients
- Communicate mission and accomplishments to the public
- Assess community needs
- Collaborate with community agencies
- Raise money
- Review (and worry) about finances
- Keep the agency afloat
- Grow the agency
- Manage facilities
- Solve technology problems
- Study and implement proper human resource regulations and policies
- Clean the office (as needed)
- Additional responsibilities as required

Special Qualifications

- Must understand and empathize with a variety of stakeholders
- Must shift priorities depending on who needs what and when
- Must creatively solve complex problems
- Must accomplish plans and objectives while dealing with emergencies

This job description describes the all-encompassing, constant, and varying demands placed on an executive director.

The challenge for me is balancing internal, operational demands with the external activities required to sustain the organization. I need to manage my schedule to be on the inside and outside at the same time.

For me, that meant concretely defining my roles and responsibilities. I revised the existing job description to better focus on the agency's priorities —short-term survival and long-term viability. (I talk more about setting priorities in the next section.) What I came up with is:

Executive Director Job Description

The executive director is the agency's public and administrative leader, overseeing day-to-day operations, managing financial obligations, engaging in long-term and strategic planning, increasing net revenues, developing and reconciling budgets, and managing marketing and resource development.

Operations

Governance

- Sit on the board of trustees, ex officio. Attend all board meetings.
- Prepare board agendas with board president. Provide regular agency updates.
- Assist board in identifying, recruiting, and interviewing potential board members.

Financial Management

- Develop and implement the annual budget. Monitor cash flow.
- Manage agency costs.
- Ensure timely meeting of all agency financial obligations.
- Oversee equipment purchase or rental.
- Oversee all financial operations, including the bookkeeping system and annual audit.
- Protect all assets by ensuring proper insurance coverage.

Human Resources

- Implement approved personnel policies and procedures. Revise as necessary.
- Recruit and train staff as needed.
- Supervise staff.
- Evaluate staff performance.

Volunteers

- Maintain volunteer recruitment channels. Serve as liaison to community organizations.
- Implement volunteer policies and procedures manual. Revise as necessary.
- Ensure adequate training and supervision of volunteers.
- Oversee volunteer retention efforts.

IT

- Oversee technological and technical functions, including implementation and use of telephone, computer, data management, and security systems.

Legal

- Act on the agency's behalf in signing all necessary papers to conduct daily business.
- Ensure that all agency legal obligations are met, including reports to regulatory bodies.

Planning

- Engage in strategic planning.
- Implement strategic plan.
- Develop and implement annual agency strategic dashboard.
- Prepare annual agency cash flow projections.

Resource Development

- Identify, research, and cultivate individual, foundation, and corporate donors.
- Increase number of contributors.
- Increase net revenues.
- Implement special events.
- Implement holiday and spring appeals.

Marketing

- Act as liaison to government, faith-based, civic, educational, business, and other nonprofit organizations within service area.
- Initiate and establish relationships with additional faith-based, civic, educational, business, and other nonprofit organizations within service area to help fulfill the organization's mission. Build collaborative partnerships.
- Develop partnerships with local, regional, and state governmental bodies and advocate for legislation that promotes the agency's mission.
- Serve as liaison to national accrediting bodies, industry associations, and peer organizations.
- Garner media coverage.

Notice the balance between internal and external activities.

I am responsible for making sure organizational operations flow smoothly. This is where most of the agency's resources are allocated, but this is *not* where my energies are focused. Most of my time is spent managing finances, laying the foundation for resource development, and representing the agency to the community. I have staff to help me run operations, and I can delegate day-to-day tasks. What I can't delegate is my role as the organization's chief representative. Executive directors are often seen as extensions of their agencies, without identities of their own. Many nonprofits, especially ones run by founders, are almost synonymous with their leaders.

Executive directors are the ones who obligate the agency, direct its activities, and allocate its resources. They are responsible for guaranteeing organizational performance. If outside people or organizations want to ensure adherence to organizational agreements, they will want to deal with the executive director. Major donors need to meet the executive director. Governmental funding agencies want their biography. Some funders require specific staff members to report directly to the executive director. Executive leadership establishes credibility with business partners, such as banks and corporations. The executive director has the ultimate responsibility and authority to get things done.

With the many internal emergencies that demand my attention, it's not always easy to maintain this external focus. To succeed at both, I have to prioritize my time and delegate what I can.

Prioritizing Tasks

To prevent myself from being pulled in all directions all the time, I needed focus. If I didn't prioritize my tasks, I would get swallowed up in the chaos and get nothing done.

I focused on my two main concerns: short-term survival and long-term sustainability. These concerns outweighed everything else, including people understanding my actions, agreeing with me or even liking what I was doing. We were in crisis. I needed to act fast and decisively. I didn't have time for consensus building. I had to make this organization succeed no matter what.

I sorted my daily activities under one of these two umbrellas. If a task didn't fit this framework, my staff and I stopped doing it.

If we didn't get through the short-term, there would be no long-term to worry about. But, if I spent all my time on the immediate problems, we would just go from crisis to crisis and never find stability. I decided to spend 70 percent of my time addressing the current crisis and 30 percent building long-term viability.

When I first started, the most immediate crisis was financial. Because of the lengthy leadership transition, the agency had not brought in enough revenue to sustain operations. The main problem was not excessive costs, but lack of income.

In my first three months, there wasn't much I could do about costs or revenues. Most of the grants scheduled to come in by year-end had already been submitted. Planning for the gala was well underway: I accepted the position August 29, my first day was October 10, the gala was November 10. The holiday appeal was the only thing that hadn't been done. So, in my first three months, all I could do to bolster short-term income was write a few grants, keep pushing the gala along, and prepare the holiday appeal. Along with board meetings, staff supervision, and getting to know the volunteers, overseeing the last fiscal quarter's fundraising activities took about 70 percent of my time.

> How you divide your time between fulfilling short-term and long-term goals will vary, depending on your organization's situation and issues.
>
> **food for thought**

The other 30 percent was spent laying the groundwork for the next fiscal year. Soon after the gala, we would need to deploy revenue-generating and cost-cutting measures to ensure our survival. I reviewed vendor contracts and sought other bids. In the New Year, I compared bids, analyzed their costs and benefits, and selected vendors.

I also developed the annual goals and objectives. Since our costs were not excessive, and I wouldn't be able to cut them enough to balance the budget, I would need to generate significant revenue. I created a development plan with revenue projections and a time line. (I talk more about creating a development plan in **Chapter Seven**.) Since fundraising is about a twelve- to fifteen-month cycle, I would have to cut expenses while waiting for my efforts to produce revenue.

Since we are mainly a volunteer-staffed organization, I would also need to concentrate on recruiting, training, and managing volunteers. Since I had staff to help me, my job was to evaluate the volunteer support structure, revise as necessary, and communicate it to staff and volunteers. Since my staff supported the volunteers, I also needed to address personnel policies, staff structure, and evaluation.

I laid out all of these priorities as objectives, which were specific, measurable, and time-oriented. Beside each objective, I listed the activities we would undertake to meet them. Beside each activity, I listed the resources we had to implement it. My original plan looked something like the following:

Sample Annual Goals and Objectives

Objective	Methodology	Resources
Increase 2012 net income by $50,000	Annual Appeal — $20,000 Foundation Revenue — $100,000 Corporate Support — $12,500 Gala — $100,000 Cash for Gold — $1,000 Major Gifts — $50,000	ED's Development background Multiple vendor options
Increase number of calls answered by 10 percent over 2011	Articulate and implement volunteer recruitment plan Improve volunteer retention Improve shift coverage Develop call centers	Experienced director of programs Untapped geographic and volunteer markets Existing relationship with Rutgers University and Caldwell College
Develop and implement a teen suicide prevention program by March 2012.	Develop relationship with schools Develop relationships with legislators Develop relationships with youth-serving, community based organizations	Suicide awareness legislation: two-hour mandatory school in-service Legislators willing to put resources behind issue Good working relationship among providers in Union County; partnership with Prevention Links and Family and Children's Services
Strengthen organizational structure to better meet mission and goals	Revise staff and volunteer job descriptions Revise employee manual Review chart of accounts Maintain regular agency-wide communications Increase press coverage	Existing HR documents Existing agency-wide staff and volunteer database ED's previous relationship with experienced PR vendor

By doing this, I created a road map so that everyone—me, the board, my staff—knew what we needed to accomplish. We knew our goals and how we would measure progress. We had a guide to make decisions when new possibilities came our way. This document was invaluable.

In addition to guiding our activities, the board also used the chart to measure my performance. We had set the goals together. Having clear benchmarks helped them decide where to shore up our efforts and what to leave alone. In addition to staff behavior, the document helped guide board behavior.

It was easy to document performance by adding a fourth column with the headings: As of First Quarter, As of Second Quarter, and so on. Documenting which objectives we had or had not met helped me prioritize and balance between short-term and long-term activities.

Delegating to Others

One person can't do everything. In fact, if you accept grants or governmental funding, you will need an outside financial audit. Part of that audit is making sure the agency follows adequate internal controls with appropriate segregation of duties. In other words, you need at least two people to carry out your financial duties, which means delegate.

> An audit is an examination of records to verify their accuracy. Outside financial audits, required by many funders, are conducted by third-party audit firms.
>
> Internal controls are a coordinated system of procedures and techniques to safeguard a company's assets, ensure the accuracy of its accounting records, and promote efficiency and adherence to prescribed policies.
>
> definition

Delegation is sometimes difficult for executive directors, but it is necessary.

To delegate successfully, I must have good communication skills. Be specific. I have to describe what I want done, the cost, the timeframe, and other parameters so that someone else understands me completely. The larger my staff, and more layers between me and my line workers, the greater the chance my message will be garbled. Ever play telephone when you were a kid? One person whispers a message to a second person, who whispers it to a third person, and so on until the end of the chain. The final person delivers the message, which is invariably different from the original one. Communicating through an organization is a lot like that.

So that everyone is on the same page, I write important communications down. Job descriptions, employee policies, operational and financial procedures, meeting agendas, meeting minutes—I commit all to writing. If I have policies or procedures that a group of people must understand and follow, I write them down and communicate them widely.

> During my first year, I rebuilt our staff structure. However, not all volunteers understood what the new staff roles were. For example, I interpreted my job responsibilities very differently than my predecessor. Many of the volunteers would see me working hard but had no idea what I was doing. As we hired new staff, volunteers had questions about who did what and who should be their contact. To make sure our volunteers were well-informed, and could see how each role fit into the big picture, I shared everyone's job descriptions, including mine. It was important information that helped everyone see how they are part of a big team.
>
> **Lessons Learned**

When I delegate, I must trust that the person performing the task has the necessary skills. However, I don't know that person's full capabilities until they reach their limit. The only way to know they have reached their limit is to give them more responsibility until they fail.

Failure is a scary proposition for executives. It might mean a deal not going through, extra costs, an interruption in operations, or an important relationship is not cultivated correctly. Failure has unpleasant consequences. But people usually learn far more from failures than successes. Letting them take risks might be worth it in the long run.

When people fail in their tasks, I look at the reasons. Did the structure I implemented prevent them from doing their job? Did I give them inconsistent messages? Did they really understand me? Were they adequately trained? Most people want to do a good job and will, if given the opportunity. Usually, people do not fulfill expectations because there has been a miscommunication or a roadblock preventing their success. So I look at what caused the failure and what I can do to keep it from repeating.

> I once worked for an organization that was constantly prodding its employees to think for themselves and solve problems on their own. At the same time, their evaluation mechanisms focused on what they did wrong.
>
> The result? Employees didn't feel safe taking risks, because they might be punished, and went to their managers for every little decision. This process was a complete drain on management and a poor use of staff resources.
>
> **stories from the real world**

Strong communication skills have helped me delegate successfully to staff and volunteers. I write important policies and procedures down, use the feedback loop, and provide consistent messaging. I have found that any steps I take to improve my communication skills are worth the effort. (For more information about communication theory, see my book *Power Your Organization's Fundraising: How the Partnership Paradigm Will Change Everything*.)

One of the attributes that helped me delegate was self-awareness. I knew what I did well, and what I did poorly. This understanding helped me form a team and know who to ask for what. I had also explored my risk tolerance, which helped me recognize how much I could comfortably delegate to someone based on their chances of success or failure. My self-awareness was invaluable. (I talk more about the role of self-awareness in **Chapter Eleven**.)

The executive director role is frenetic and all-encompassing. Structure your work to fulfill all your responsibilities as the organization's chief representative, focusing on both the internal and external environments. Prioritize your tasks to meet both short-term and long-term objectives. Delegate whenever you can. Everything will demand your attention if you let it—don't let it.

To Recap

- Balance internal, operational demands on your time with crucial external activities.
- Prioritize your tasks by creating only a few objectives that support both long-term and short-term goals.
- Delegate when you can.

Chapter Six

Financial Management

IN THIS CHAPTER

- The importance of mission focus
- Finances as an expression of organizational values
- Managing revenues, expenses, and cash flow
- Getting the most bang for your buck

Let me start by admitting I am not a financial guru, accountant, economist, or financial planner. I don't have to be. I do have some training in financial management. To augment that training, I read, attend seminars, and ask questions. As an executive director, it's important for me to understand where my organization's resources are coming from, where they are going, and when. Those are the basics. Successfully generating and managing resources allows my nonprofit to fulfill its mission.

The Importance of a Mission Focus

It's easy to think of resource generation and management in terms of organizational needs: to cover costs, we need so much revenue.

But a nonprofit survives on donations, and donors don't really care about organizational survival except to fulfill the mission. You do not raise money to survive as an organization; you raise money to serve your mission. (I talk more about revenue generation in **Chapter Seven**.)

In resource development for more than twenty years, I have learned that everything I communicate about my organization's finances must tie into my organization's mission and how well we are meeting it. Do we make it clear that donations to us are being used prudently to support the mission? For example, what is our overhead rate? How does that compare with our industry's average? How is executive compensation determined? Are we in line with similar nonprofits? Do we have an outside audit done each year? Can we prove that our resources are being used properly? Do we publish an annual report, including financial statements? Do we publish financial information on our website?

I communicate the relationship between resource management and mission fulfillment with charts and graphs. These visual representations make it easy for people to comprehend where their money is going and how it is being used. Simple charts look something like this:

Sample Revenue Pie Chart

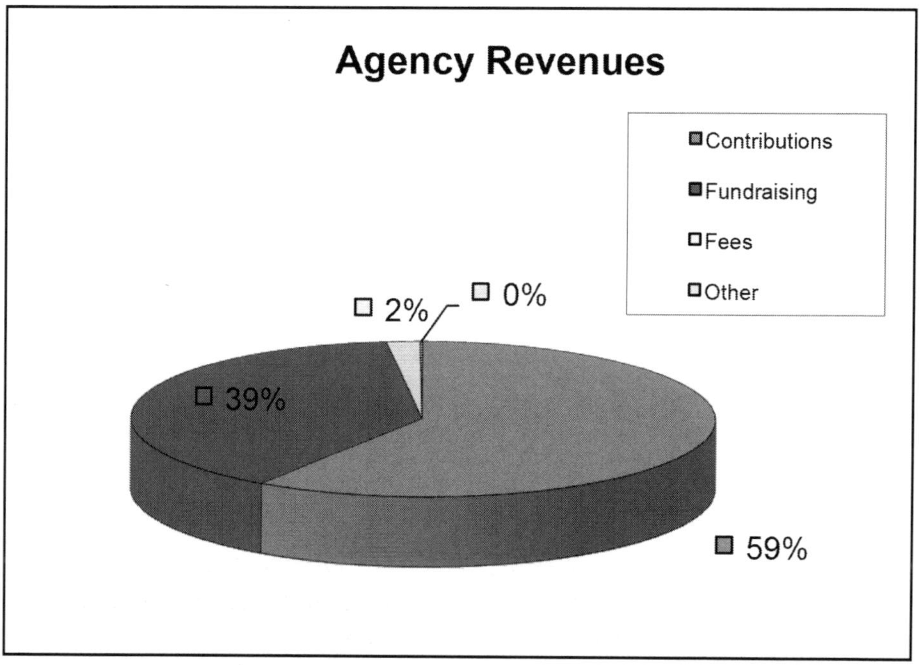

Sample Expense Pie Chart

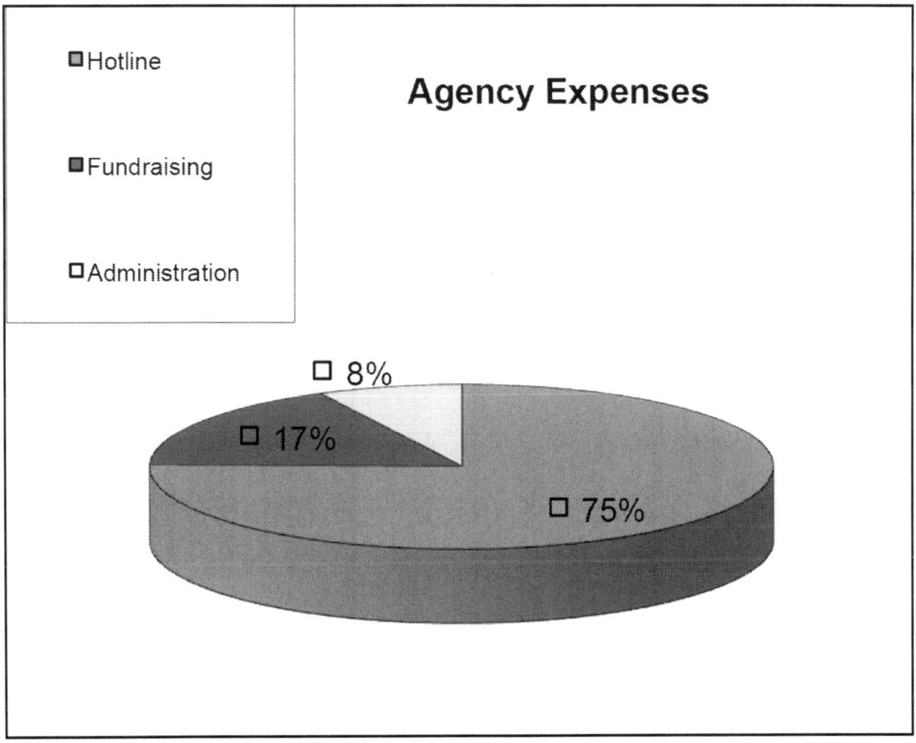

Sample Financial Trends Bar Graph

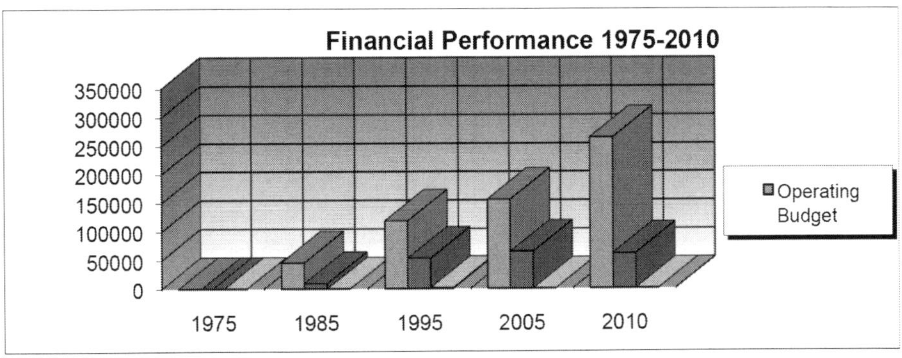

The revenue chart shows that much of the agency's revenue comes from donations. You can also see that most of the expenses are spent on programs, in this case a hotline. The trend chart shows that revenues have steadily increased over the life of the agency. Assets increased until 2005, when they started to level off. Liabilities remain nil.

Assets are the value of properties, tangible and intangible, that an organization owns. Assets can include cash, stock, equipment, real estate, receivables, and goodwill.

Liabilities are debts or financial obligations.

definition

The charts show a steady increase in income and assets, with no liabilities. Combined with healthy service growth, this metric makes a powerful statement on mission growth and fulfillment.

Finances as an Expression of Organizational Values

Resource allocation decisions are value decisions. How we spend our money tells others what is important to us. Therefore, the costs I incur need to result from deliberate decisions, not haphazard line items that are there because they've always been. The methods I use to generate revenue must relate to my mission. I don't endorse activities just to raise money. There might be nothing wrong with the budgets I inherited; however, it was worth examining how those budgets communicated organizational values.

For example, recruiting, training, managing, and retaining volunteers are high priorities for me. I value my volunteers and want to meet their needs. So, one of my personnel line items is a volunteer manager, dedicated solely to supporting our volunteers. I also invest in volunteer support items, like snacks and water for long shifts. In addition, I hold a volunteer dinner every year, so volunteer appreciation is also a line item. I value my volunteers, and it shows in my budget.

The values in your budget must be reflected throughout your organization. For example, if volunteer management is important, you need to fund it and employ best practices. These will be reflected in job descriptions, employee policies and procedures, and performance reviews.

practical tip

I value mission fulfillment above all else, so my revenue generating activities all have mission components. For example, my gala always includes keynote speakers who share how our mission affects them and saves lives. Our honorees are chosen because of their efforts to support the mission. I implemented a teen suicide educational campaign, which underlies many of our fundraising efforts. I only conduct revenue generating activities that relate to our mission. (I talk more about revenue generation in **Chapter Seven**.)

> Net income is revenues minus expenses. A positive net income means you have more revenues than expenses. A negative net income means you have more expenses than revenues.
>
> definition

When I design my budget, looking at revenues and expenses, I analyze each item in terms of mission and whether it is a worthy task. I use mission and values to decide what the budget will look like.

Managing Revenues, Expenses, and Cash Flow

When I was a development director, I created expense budgets and revenue and expense budgets all the time. My main concern was showing a positive net income, i.e., ensuring that revenues equaled or exceeded expenses. I really didn't worry about cash flow, except as it related to program implementation: when funding would start, when it would end, and when I would have to find new money. My world revolved around net income.

Now that I am an executive director, I speak a whole new language called cash flow. Our annual budget shows a positive net income. That's a good thing. But if you look at when the revenue comes in and when the bills need to be paid, very few months have a positive net income. Managing when money comes and goes out is a new world.

Managing Expenses

Expenses are easier to manage than revenues. They are much more predictable from month to month. For example, employees get paid according to a schedule, rent and telephone bills are paid monthly, and office supply bills are pretty constant. Regular expenses like these are steady and ongoing. And, with occasional exceptions, they are pretty much the same amount.

Even when expenses aren't so steady, they might be predictable. Take insurance premiums. Mine are due when the policies renew, not in monthly installments. They are not regular and steady, but I know when they are due and how much they will be. Another example is gala expenses. I only incur the costs once a year, but I know how much and when.

So predicting my monthly expenses is fairly easy, and my monthly cost budgets tend to be predictable. Look at the sample annual and monthly cost budgets below.

Sample Annual Cost Budget

Expenses	
Salaries and Wages	$300,000
Professional Fees	$24,000
Rent	$24,000
Telecommunications	$8,400
Equipment	$5,000
Insurance	$8,500
Special Event Expenses	$25,000
Printing and Outreach	$5,000
All other (postage, supplies, travel, dues, cleaning)	$14,500
Total Expenses	$414,400

Sample Annual Cost Budget by Month

*Columns may not add exactly due to rounding

Expenses	Jan	Feb	Mar	Apr	May	Jun
Salaries and Wages	25,000	25,000	25,000	25,000	25,000	25,000
Professional Fees	1,000	1,000	4,000	4,000	3,000	3,000
Rent	2,000	2,000	2,000	2,000	2,000	2,000
Telecommunications	700	700	700	700	700	700
Equipment	417	417	417	417	417	417
Insurance	3,550	2,000	0	2,100	0	0
Special Event Expenses	0	2,500	2,500	1,500	1,500	1,500
Printing and Outreach	417	417	417	417	417	417
All other	1,208	1,208	1,208	1,208	1,208	1,208
Total Expenses	34,242	35,242	36,242	37,342	34,242	34,242

Expenses	Jul	Aug	Sep	Oct	Nov	Dec
Salaries and Wages	25,000	25,000	25,000	25,000	25,000	25,000
Professional Fees	1,000	1,000	1,000	1,000	1,000	3,000
Rent	2,000	2,000	2,000	2,000	2,000	2,000
Telecommunications	700	700	700	700	700	700
Equipment	417	417	417	417	417	417
Insurance	0	850	0	0	0	0
Special Event Expenses	1,500	1,500	3,000	7,500	3,000	0
Printing and Outreach	417	417	417	417	417	417
All other	1,208	1,208	1,208	1,208	1,208	1,208
Total Expenses	32,242	33,092	33,742	38,242	33,742	32,742

Notice the relative stability of the monthly cash output, hovering between $32,000 and $38,000.

Managing Revenues

Managing revenues is trickier than managing expenses, largely because revenues are not as steady or predictable as costs. This has been one of the hardest parts of managing our finances, and I haven't always gotten it right. Sometimes money comes in early, late, or not in the amount I predicted.

The tables below show what a sample annual revenue budget might look like, along with a corresponding projection of when those revenues might be realized.

Sample Annual Revenue Budget

Revenues	
General Donations	$100,000
Foundations and Civic	$50,000
Corporate Contributions	$10,000
Special Events	$85,000
Program Fees	$5,000
Government	$200,000
Total Revenues	$450,000

Sample Annual Revenue Budget by Month

*Columns may not add exactly due to rounding

Revenues	Jan	Feb	Mar	Apr	May	Jun
General Donations	5,000	4,000	3,500	10,000	15,000	3,500
Foundations and Civic	8,000	2,000	2,500	2,500	5,000	7,500
Corporate Contributions	0	500	1,000	1,000	500	500
Special Events	0	1,500	1,800	3,500	0	1,200
Program Fees	500	700	500	150	300	300
Government	16,667	16,667	16,667	16,667	16,667	16,667
Total Revenues	30,107	25,367	25,967	33,817	37,467	29,667

Revenues	Jul	Aug	Sep	Oct	Nov	Dec
General Donations	2,000	1,000	2,000	2,000	17,000	35,000
Foundations and Civic	0	0	0	5,000	7,500	10,000
Corporate Contributions	500	500	1,000	1,500	1,500	1,500
Special Events	10,000	0	32,000	35,000	0	0
Program Fees	100	550	1,000	500	1,000	0
Government	16,667	16,667	16,667	16,667	16,667	16,667
Total Revenues	29,267	18,717	52,667	60,667	43,667	63,167

Notice how much more variation there is in this monthly projection, as compared to the monthly expense projection. With monthly expenses, we are between $32,000 and $38,000; with revenues we were between $17,000 and $63,000. Money does not come in at the same rate it goes out. This uneven revenue stream has major implications for your resource development plan.

These figures mean nothing without the cost picture. To know how much revenue to raise, you must know your costs. If you don't raise at least enough money to meet costs, the organization becomes financially vulnerable. Always do your cost budget first, using it as a basis for your revenue budget.

If you rely on grants and special events to meet your budget, you must come to terms with steady costs and a relatively unsteady revenue stream, which brings me to cash flow.

Managing Cash Flow

I was on the job less than a month when I presented my first annual revenue, expense and cash flow budgets to the board. These budgets made several assumptions about revenues and expenses that just weren't true. I presented a very rosy budget based on the stretch goals I had made for myself and the agency.

Wrong thing to do. By presenting a stretch budget, I set expectations too high. Also, there was no way for the board to know our financial situation if I didn't meet my goals. I would have been much better off presenting more realistic annual and cash flow budgets. Of course, because of all the transition, the previous year had not been typical. I was flying blind, and I hadn't been there long enough to know my assumptions were off. It was a big lesson.

Putting together the above monthly revenue and expense annual budgets and monthly cash flow projections, we get a monthly net income analysis that looks like this:

Sample Annual Revenue and Expense Budget

Revenues	$450,000
Expenses	$414,400
Net Income	$35,600

Sample Monthly Net Income Projections

*Columns may not add exactly due to rounding

	Jan	Feb	March	April	May	Jun
Revenues	30,107	25,367	25,967	33,817	37,467	29,667
Expenses	34,242	35,242	36,242	37,342	34,242	34,242
Net Income	(4,135)	(9,875)	(10,275)	(3,525)	3,225	(4,575)

	Jul	Aug	Sep	Oct	Nov	Dec
Revenues	29,267	18,717	52,667	60,667	43,667	63,167
Expenses	32,242	33,092	33,742	38,242	33,742	32,742
Net Income	(2,975)	(14,375)	18,925	22,425	9,925	26,375

With the annual budget, we end the year with positive net revenue. The same is not true month by month. Notice how many months there is negative net income—seven out of twelve. To get through these months, I need enough reserves at the beginning of the year to carry me through, to implement another revenue generating activity earlier in the year, to move expenses toward the end of the year, or to tap into other sources of capital, such as a loan or line of credit.

Look at what happens to cash flow if I begin the year with a $40,000 balance.

Sample Monthly Cash Flow Projection #1

	Beginning Balance	Jan	Feb	Mar	Apr	May	Jun
Net Income		(4,135)	(9,875)	(10,275)	(3,525)	3,225	(4,575)
Cash Flow	40,000	35,865	25,990	15,715	12,190	15,415	10,840

	Beginning Balance	Jul	Aug	Sep	Oct	Nov	Dec
Net Income		(2,975)	(14,375)	18,925	22,425	9,925	26,375
Cash Flow	40,000	7,865	(6,510)	12,415	34,840	44,765	71,140

Although my end-of-year cash balance is a very healthy $75,600, I don't make it through the year. My cash runs out in August and I can't pay the bills. Even before then, I am cutting it very close. What happens if my revenues come in later or lower than expected? What if I incur an unexpected cost?

Now notice what happens with a $75,000 beginning balance.

Sample Monthly Cash Flow Projection #2

	Beginning Balance	Jan	Feb	Mar	Apr	May	Jun
Net Income		(4,135)	(9,875)	(10,275)	(3,525)	3,225	(4,575)
Cash Flow	75,000	70,865	60,990	50,715	47,190	50,415	45,840

	Beginning Balance	Jul	Aug	Sep	Oct	Nov	Dec
Net Income		(2,975)	(14,375)	18,925	22,425	9,925	26,375
Cash Flow	75,000	42,865	28,490	47,415	69.480	79,765	106,140

I'm okay through the whole year. Even though net income might be negative during some months, my cash flow stays positive.

This is why cash reserves and endowments are so important. You need something to get you through the lean times. Cash reserves can help you during the negative net income months and endowments can be used as collateral for loans.

> Many times, overhead or indirect expenses are not allowed in grant budgets, particularly government ones. In that case, you will need to include percentages of your indirect costs as part of your direct cost budget.
>
> practical tip

Getting the Most Bang for Your Buck

Here, I briefly discuss the financial concepts I consider when making revenue decisions. For a more in-depth discussion, and examples on how to calculate these financial ratios, see my book *Succeed in Your Nonprofit Funding Partnerships: Analyzing Their Costs and Benefits.*

Taking Total Costs into Account

> **Return on Investment**
>
> Return on investment is a performance measure used to evaluate the efficiency of an investment. Financial return on investment is calculated as net income divided by costs and is useful to compare the financial efficacy of one activity over another. In addition to financial return on investment, nonprofits must also consider mission return on investment.
>
> definition

When looking at the total agency budget, I deal with all of my line items, i.e., my total revenues and costs. However, when formulating program, event, and grant budgets I won't necessarily use all my line items—only those relevant to the specific program, event, or grant I am considering. However, I still have to pay those costs, whether they are budgeted or not.

For example, in a training budget, it's very easy to include the direct costs for instructors and training manuals. It's more difficult to remember a portion of the executive director, rental, phone,

> **Sample Return on Investment Comparisons**
>
> (Total Revenues – Total Expenses)/Total Expenses = Return on Investment
>
> Total Gala Revenues: $100,000
>
> Total Gala Expenses: $40,000
>
> (100,000 – 40,000)/40,000 = 150 percent Gala Return on Investment
>
> Total Annual Appeal Revenues: $50,000
>
> Total Annual Appeal Expenses: $7,500
>
> (50,000 – 7,500)/7,500 = 567 percent Annual Appeal Return on Investment
>
> Total Grantwriting Revenues: $200,000
>
> Total Grantwriting Expenses: $57,200
>
> (200,000 – 57,200)/57,200 = 249.6 percent Grantwriting Return on Investment
>
> **Example**

and other indirect costs. Quite often, someone does not take indirect expenses into account when planning a program, event, or grant budget. As a result, they don't raise enough to cover total costs. Always remember to include both direct and indirect costs in your budget calculations.

Return on investment is net income divided by total costs. The return on investment ratio tells you how well your money is working for you. It lets you know how much revenue you generate from a specific activity for every dollar you invest. This ratio is particularly helpful when you have to make choices. For example, you can compare the return on investment for growing your gala to putting more resources into grantwriting or expanding your annual appeal. Maybe you don't want to invest in fundraising activities at all but would rather put money in traditional investments. Your decision will not rest solely on the financial return from the investment, but it should be a factor.

> **Profit Margin**
>
> Profit margin measures profitability by calculating net income divided by revenues. This ratio shows how much our revenue exceeds our costs. Nonprofits must reinvest all profits into the mission, rather than distributing them to owners or shareholders.
>
> definition

In the following example, you get the best return on investment from your annual appeal. From a purely financial standpoint, it makes sense to grow your annual appeal, rather than the gala or grantwriting.

I don't recommend putting all your efforts into one activity. For example, a gala provides nonfinancial returns on investment, such as community visibility and partnership building. These benefits are measured by financial return on investment. Grantwriting will help you reach a different audience than a gala or direct mail. However, if you have all the revenue streams you want and must choose where to invest, the annual appeal generates the best return on investment.

Profit margin is net income divided by total revenues and is highly related to return on investment. This metric lets you see what percentage of gross revenues produced by an activity are actually profit. I find this useful when deciding which activities to undertake. It's also helpful when comparing more mission-related programs that generate little profit with higher profit activities. If I need a certain amount of net income by the end of the year to build up cash reserves or add to an endowment, I need to balance activities that break-even against those that make money. Profit margin can tell me what I need to know.

Sample Profit Margin Comparisons

(Total Revenues – Total Expenses)/Total Revenue = Profit Margin

Total Gala Revenues: $100,000

Total Gala Expenses: $40,000

(100,000 – 40,000)/100,000 = 60 percent Gala Profit Margin

Total Annual Appeal Revenues: $50,000

Total Annual Appeal Expenses: $7,500

(50,000 – 7,500)/50,000 = 85 percent Annual Appeal Profit Margin

Total Grantwriting Revenues: $200,000

Total Grantwriting Expenses: $57,200

(200,000 – 57,200)/200,000 = 71.4 percent Grantwriting Profit Margin

Example

In this example, you realize the best profit margin from the annual appeal, followed by grantwriting and the gala. Profit margin is very much related to return on investment.

I am not a financial guru. However, I have found that these rudimentary tools help me balance the mission with raising money. In fact, finances are a statement about my organization's values and what we consider important. Values are what guide me in fulfilling the mission. The numbers may be my least favorite part of the job, but they are crucial to moving my organization forward. I must be profitable to grow and expand the mission. And I must always remember… that the mission is our reason for existence.

To Recap

- Raise money for mission fulfillment, not organizational needs.
- Remember, your budget is an expression of organizational values.
- Manage revenues prudently.
- Manage cash flow carefully.
- Take your total costs into account.
- Calculate return on investment.
- Calculate profit margin.

Chapter Seven

Resource Development

IN THIS CHAPTER

- Revenue generation with a mission focus
- Revenue diversification
- The development plan
- The executive director's role in fundraising
- Everybody fundraises

I am a very good fundraiser. I have been in resource development for more than twenty years. I can easily write about what it takes to raise money. But this is not a chapter about fundraising, per se. It's about which skills helped me through my first year and the broader perspective I needed to succeed in my new role. For more about how to fundraise, see my book *Power Your Organization's Fundraising: How the Partnership Paradigm Will Change Everything*.

Revenue Generation with a Mission Focus

Revenue generation is *not* about money, it's about mission fulfillment. If you go after money for money's sake, in the long term, you will fail.

The board has a legal and fiduciary responsibility to carry on the organization's mission. It delegates much of that responsibility to the executive director, who must advance the agency's mission, which supersedes operations. Carrying on the mission is the overarching goal and is sometimes forgotten when we get caught up in day-to-day details.

> Fiduciary responsibility is holding something in trust for another or standing in a special relationship of trust, confidence or responsibility in certain obligations to others.
>
> definition

There are a million different fundraising activities I can implement; I choose those that relate to the mission. In the last chapter, I talked about financial return on investment. Mission return on investment is equally important.

In my annual appeal, I write about how we are meeting the community's need. At the gala, I choose themes that enhance community awareness about our work. In my search for grant funding, I pursue funders who share our goals. When I approach potential donors, I talk about how they can help fulfill the mission—I don't ask them to help the agency survive. This mission focus—helping other people live fulfilling, productive lives—is the number one reason we generate enough revenue to continue operations.

Always remember: put mission first.

Revenue Diversification

There are lots of ways to make money, and different nonprofits use different funding strategies. When I started the job, my organization had only one significant revenue stream: donations. These gifts came from individuals, donor matches, foundations, sponsorships, and ticket sales over and above the fair market value of events. Other potential income streams are governmental funding (common in human services), fee-for-service (YMCAs, child care centers, hospitals), fee-for-product (Goodwill), and endowment or investments (foundations).

Each stream requires different resources and skills to manage and produces varying income. The streams you choose depend on your organization's resources, strengths, weaknesses, opportunities, and threats. In other words, your revenue diversification plan should be determined by your strategic planning. (I talk more about strategic planning in **Chapter Ten**.)

My organization's revenue structure, which relies on donations, means we must be crackerjack fundraisers. We need people who excel at development, grantwriting, special events, and spring and holiday appeals. We also need to manage our donor database, track income, send timely thank you letters, and coordinate follow-up asks. Luckily, I am experienced at all these tasks, which makes me a good fit to oversee the revenue structure.

Different organizations need varying skill sets. Foundations, or large organizations with endowments, need a leader with legal and financial expertise. Their executive directors are preoccupied with financial markets and returns. Their boards oversee the endowment, and will be most interested in investment strategies. Even if the executive director hires an investment firm to oversee the endowment, the director still has to understand and communicate the financial ups and downs to the board. Understanding sophisticated investing takes training, and reading and deciphering financial reports takes time.

> A revenue structure is a business model that determines how the organization creates, delivers, and captures economic and social value. Revenue structures reflect how the organization's purpose, offerings, strategies, infrastructure, business practices, operational policies and procedures capture different forms of revenue. The structure reflects management's concept of what donors and funders want, how they want it, and how the organization gets paid.
>
> definition

If you have a fee-for-service or fee-for-product structure, such as selling training to businesses, you need marketing and sales skills, an infrastructure to help you research markets, training to fit market needs, marketing materials, and staff to sell the service. Instead of investing in someone with a development background, or building a whole department, you want to hire someone with a corporate sales and marketing background or develop a department around corporate research and relations.

Government funding has its own resource requirements. You need someone with public or governmental affairs expertise to build relationships with legislators. You must ramp up advocacy efforts to influence the political and budgeting processes, and you will need a skilled government grantwriter and contract negotiator to apply for funding.

If you accept government funding, you need crackerjack monitoring and reporting systems to take care of the paperwork and respond to audits. The organization must do what it promised, in the prescribed period, and prove it. And, in case the government is slow in paying because the budget is cut, funding is not renewed, or it shuts down, you will need a good backup plan. Government funding can be a godsend, helping you maintain positive cash flow. But in today's economic and political environment, it isn't always reliable.

In an article in the *Nonprofit Quarterly,* "Truth or Consequences: The Implications of Financial Decisions," Clara Miller talks about broad categories of nonprofit revenue streams: government contracts, charitable contributions (of all types: individual, foundation, and corporate), earned revenue (fees for products or services), and endowment income. She digs into how well nonprofits with single and multiple revenue streams succeed, defining success as greater profitability and liquidity (cash availability), as opposed to budget size.

Miller found that nonprofits with two main revenue streams have higher profit margins and greater liquidity than organizations with one or three. Presumably, this is because nonprofits with less than two lack flexibility, while those with more than two lose focus and misuse resources, notably staff.

The article can be found at http://www.nonprofitquarterly.org/management/20281-truth-or-consequences-the-implications-of-financial-decisions.html.

food for thought

The Development Plan

A revenue generation plan, often called a development plan, outlines your fundraising activities for the year. When you choose which fundraising activities to do, and when, you must consider both financial concerns and mission.

You do some activities because they are integral to your mission, such as advocacy campaigns. You might earn very little or even subsidize them. You might conduct other activities because they generate revenue, such as selling candy. Some activities generate revenue and create community awareness, such as a gala. These might not be the only reasons you undertake such activities, but they are certainly the main ones.

There are ways to structure fundraising activities to generate public awareness. In fact, one of the purposes for annual appeals, charity runs or galas is to raise awareness and participation. Just make sure the activity relates to your mission.

practical tip

When deciding between two actions, my first concern is mission. How does the activity further my mission? If it doesn't, I don't do it. For example, we operate a crisis hotline, it makes no sense to invest in housing and collect rents. Our mission is to provide emotional support for people experiencing crisis. We could make money in the housing market, but it would divert precious resources from our mission. We would lose our organizational identity.

When choosing which programs to implement, I factor in revenues and expenses. If I don't have the revenue to implement it, I don't do it. Also, unless I *must* do it to maintain mission viability, I won't undertake it if the costs aren't recouped. The last thing I want is recurring costs with no sustained funding.

I also consider cash flow. Positive annual net income does not always translate into positive monthly net income. We need both to survive. (See **Chapter Six** for illustrations.)

One way to bolster income during lean months is to add a fundraising activity. When I started, most of our revenue came in during the fall, but I needed more in the spring. I checked our events calendar, saw which market segments I was reaching through grants and special events, and looked at who I wasn't reaching. Only a few of our volunteer listeners attended the gala, in some cases because of the cost. So I decided to implement a volunteer-to-friend, low-ask appeal. I overestimated how much revenue it would generate in the first year, but it still did quite well. Also, my volunteers look forward to it, and I have a baseline to promote next year's appeal.

Another strategy is to build up your cash reserves or endowment. In my first year, one of my goals was to end the year with enough cash to get through the following year's lean months. It will take longer to create an endowment, on which I can take a line of credit.

> If you are initiating a new fundraiser, remember that it takes about five years to reach its income potential.
>
> practical tip

A third consideration is human resources. You can pick the most mission-related activity with the highest return on investment at the greatest profit and schedule it to bring in revenue when you need it most. But if you don't have the staff to implement it, the effort will fail. Remember, it doesn't have to be paid staff. I rely on more than a hundred volunteers. However, if they don't have the experience, or we don't have time to train them (or they don't want to do it), it's not going to get done. You have to consider staff workload and volunteer skills and preferences before implementing a new activity. Otherwise, you have a good idea with no chance of success.

The Role Executive Director's in Fundraising

Executive directors play an extremely important role in revenue generation. They lay the foundation, structure the staff, and delegate the work. Executive directors also develop the relationships.

> Planning and forethought. Always planning and forethought.
>
> important

As a former development director, I understand the executive director's role. Fundraising is about building relationships and letting people be part of a successful mission fulfillment. Part of my role is to help form those relationships. As head of a small organization, with only three paid staff (including me), I work with a special events planner and handle much of the development work myself. However, if I didn't have a fundraising background, I would need to hire a development professional.

As executive director, my primary role is to keep the focus on mission. It's easy to focus on money when I talk about raising it and how much is raised, but that is not what the organization is about. I need to constantly reinforce the message that these resources exist to fulfill the mission.

As executive director, I must interact with the outside world so people know what my organization is and why we exist. That means researching which community people and groups I want to interact with. In other words, I need to form strategic partnerships in the community. As chief organizational representative, this is not a responsibility I can delegate.

As executive director, I must encourage the board to give. Board members are the volunteers most vested in the organization. They also have to be the lead givers. I don't necessarily mean the top givers, but rather the first to give. And when they give, it should be a stretch gift. I want 100 percent board participation. As the organization's leaders, they set the example for everyone else.

> People do not give *to* organizations as much as they give *through* organizations.
>
> **Lessons Learned**

The board must help fundraise. When I started, my board made it clear they were not fundraisers and didn't have the wealthy connections to raise a lot of money. That's a common objection. To fix it, I brought them in on activities that generated revenue—I just didn't call it fundraising.

For example, at the end of the year, each board member calls donors to thank them. They also help me research and negotiate more favorable vendor contracts and make community connections. It's easy for them to do if I don't call it fundraising.

They all give, attend events, and tout the agency to friends and co-workers, who they also invite to the gala. In other words, the board is generating resources to fulfill our mission. It's my job to cultivate that.

> More and more funders are requiring 100 percent board giving.
>
> ! important

As executive director, I need to foster important donor relationships. As chief executive officer, I am the only person who can guarantee that resources are allocated to achieve a specific

Calling and thanking donors was an eye-opening experience for my board. Many of them were pleasantly surprised and motivated by the responses.

stories from the real world

outcome. Therefore, I need to participate in donor meetings, attend site visits with foundation representatives, and help cultivate major donors, assuring them their donations will be used wisely. I must actively partner with my development staff—not let them work in isolation.

Fundraising is an integral part of every executive's director job.

Everybody Fundraises: Fundraising, Branding, and Marketing

Fundraising and marketing are highly interrelated. Fundraisers sell their agency's mission and goodwill to donors. Nonprofit goods and services must be marketed to be sold. No one will buy these products without a guarantee they are getting good value: that feeling of doing good, a cleaner environment, a child's swim lesson, or a heart transplant. Your brand is measured by how well your products meet your donor's or client's expectations. The better your brand, the more you'll sell.

Nonprofit marketing is the process of creating, communicating, delivering, and exchanging goods or services that have value for donors, funders, clients, partners, and society at large.

A brand is the public's perception of how well an individual, organization or product meets its promises. A nonprofit's brand is based on how well the agency meets its mission.

Branding is the process of building up an individual's, organization's or product's reputation.

definition

Your brand is your reputation. Everyone in your organization contributes to that reputation. The receptionist is probably the first point of contact for clients. How that receptionist answers the phone contributes to your brand. Program staff and volunteers deliver your services. How well they treat clients also contributes to your brand. The development staff interacts with donors. Their ability to meet your donors' needs affects your brand. In short, anyone who has anything to do with the organization's operations impacts the brand. Since branding is such an integral part of marketing and fundraising, anyone who has anything to do with operations contributes to your ability to raise revenue.

Teach your brand to everyone in the organization. In the nonprofit world, we call this communicating and infusing vision. In addition to training staff and volunteers to do their jobs, you must also stress their roles as agency ambassadors. Every staff member contributes to revenue generation. As a result, meeting staff needs, as well as those of donors and volunteers, is also part of your brand. Because you have authority over the resources your people help generate, you have a responsibility to show them those resources are being used wisely.

Let everyone know how they contribute to organizational success. Nobody at the top—you, the development director, the marketing director—is generating all the resources to fulfill the mission, the people on the front lines are. If you plan and execute a terrific gala, but have dissatisfied clients, you won't fare well in the long term. We all market. We all fundraise. We build our brand together.

> Embracing the mantra "everybody fundraises" has helped me change my agency's fundraising culture and infuse vision throughout the organization. Everybody is an active participant.
>
> **Lessons Learned**

Different agencies have different funding streams. While developing your revenue plan, you need to consider expenses, cash flow, and human resources when choosing activities. However, whatever you decide, always let mission be your primary motivator. It's easy to get caught up in revenue for revenue's sake. After all, the organization has needs. But that is not the point of nonprofit fundraising. It's *not* about the money or organizational needs; it's about fulfilling the mission.

To Recap

- Don't fundraise to raise money, fundraise to further the mission.
- Know your organization's resources, strengths, opportunities, and threats to determine ideal revenue streams.
- Take both mission and financial performance into account when choosing one revenue-generating activity over another.
- Remember your role in fundraising.
- Get everyone involved in fundraising, marketing, and branding.

Chapter Eight

Working with Staff and Volunteers

IN THIS CHAPTER

- ···➔ Defining roles and responsibilities
- ···➔ Motivating staff and volunteers
- ···➔ Staff development
- ···➔ Keeping communication open

There is no way one person can run a nonprofit alone. By law, to be a 501(c)(3), you must have a board of directors. Also, if you want to pursue government and most foundation funding, you will need an annual outside audit and appropriate internal controls to segregate duties. The nonprofit legal structure demands collaboration.

The board is the governance team. Now, let's focus on the operational team, the staff and volunteers who carry out your day-to-day programs.

Defining Roles and Responsibilities

My relationship with the board is multi-faceted and complicated. This is not the case with my staff and volunteers. I am the chief executive officer, the person in charge, the final decision-maker, the boss. There is absolutely no role confusion, unless I allow it.

I didn't allow any confusion about my role. After my budget process was done, and I developed an annual plan, I clarified roles and responsibilities.

Executive directors can create confusion about their jobs if they do not embrace their leadership role, waffle on decisions, change their minds frequently, fail to exercise their authority, or communicate inconsistently.

food for thought

I inherited a training director, clinical director, office manager, and more than a hundred volunteer listeners. I interpreted my role very differently from my predecessor. In addition, the staff had experienced four different executive directors in the previous year. They didn't know which way was up. I needed to let them know, quickly, what I wanted from them and how we fit together as a team.

I worked on job descriptions, looked at what the organization needed to accomplish, learned what my volunteer listeners and staff brought to the table, and refined their roles. My listeners answered phones and helped callers. My training director implemented volunteer training. My clinical director managed clinical support. My office manager made sure all office, equipment, and facility needs were met.

In addition to the leadership crisis, we were facing a financial crisis. The organization couldn't sustain all staff positions and survive. We had to downsize.

Layoffs, reorganizations, acquisitions, and mergers almost always require changes in roles and responsibilities.

observation

My first step was to evaluate how much clerical support we needed with only three program staff. I cut those hours first. Eventually, I needed to cut a position and chose the clinical director. But I still needed non-clinical volunteer support. So I cut the clinical director position and increased the training director's hours, promoting her to director of programs. Within six months, the office manager told me she was looking for another job, and I decided not to replace her. Down to two staff and more than a hundred volunteers, we needed to define roles and work together as a team.

The first job description I tackled was for the volunteer listener. Fortunately, it only needed minor tweaking. To make sure everyone was on the same page, I shared that description with all volunteers and staff.

I also looked at when I could hire someone to help my director of programs. I asked for her input about what the agency needed to accomplish. I outlined my perceptions of both our jobs, again, with her input. We defined our roles by putting external relationships in my bucket and internal in hers. I would develop the relationships and secure the resources she needed to implement operations. She would make sure operations ran smoothly. I refined my description with the board and shared it with her. Together, we tackled her job description. In the end, we both knew how our respective responsibilities contributed to organizational success.

> Cutting hours and laying people off are two of the hardest things an executive director will ever have to do.
>
> **Lessons Learned**

Then came time to add staff. The director of programs and I looked at what we wanted the organization to accomplish and talked about our respective needs. We came up with a job description for a volunteer manager, who would support the volunteers and report to the director of programs. This freed the director of programs to recruit new volunteers, oversee interns and perform other key functions.

I now had four job descriptions: executive director, volunteer listener, director of programs, and volunteer manager. However, the volunteers were confused about who did what. Several volunteers commented that they saw me working hard but had no idea what I was doing. To remedy this, I sent all job descriptions to the entire organization: board, staff, and volunteers. Everyone could see our roles and how we fit together as a team,

With clearly outlined roles and responsibilities, people felt more secure. In spite of the changes, we were moving forward and they were an important part of the team. Defining roles helped everyone know how to contribute to our mission.

> In times of change, people need something steady to cling to. The more definitive I am about what I need them to do, and how they are part of a bigger whole, the better off I'll be.
>
> **Lessons Learned**

Motivating Staff and Volunteers

People are the best resource to fulfill the mission. Our people carry the organization's message, fulfill its missions, and connect to the community. We can't succeed without their help. We have to cultivate our human resources.

People need to feel they are part of something bigger and their contributions are appreciated. Whether a donor, employee or volunteer, they work for, and give to, nonprofits to make a difference in the world.

Working with Volunteers

When we think of volunteers, we implicitly understand their importance. They freely give their time, talent, and treasure. We are grateful for the tasks they carry out and how they moderate our workload and add to our resource base. Working with volunteers can be one of the most rewarding experiences a nonprofit staffer can have.

Volunteers can be the lifeblood of an agency, but they need to be managed and supported correctly. Volunteers need as much role definition as paid staff, including job descriptions and training. If you haven't already, implement an orientation and training program.

People need to be validated for their contributions, and they need to be corrected when they make mistakes. Volunteers are no exception. Hold them accountable for their actions and gently guide them through trouble. Have them report to someone and meet with them to talk about performance. Constantly thank them for their gifts of time and talent, and reward them for a job well done. Set up a leadership structure they can grow into as they seek greater challenges. Volunteers need the same job structure as employees. They are, after all, staff—they just aren't paid staff. Give them what they need and show them how they contribute to the greater good.

Working with Staff

Sometimes we take our paid staff for granted. We expect them to do what they're told, carry out their responsibilities, embrace the mission, represent the organization positively, and appreciate their paychecks.

> Remember that your volunteers are unpaid staff—emphasis on the word "staff."
>
> ! important

Employees are just as valuable as volunteers. Good employees are worth their weight in gold. Remember, your employees can work at any number of agencies, but they choose yours. They could work at a for-profit, instead of a nonprofit—and it's not for the pay. Compared to the for-profit world, nonprofits are notorious for offering lower salaries. Nonprofit staff has the same motivations as volunteers: they want to contribute to the greater good and make a difference in the world.

As chief of staff, it's important to recognize the gifts and talents my employees give me. Pay is not going to be their number one motivator. They need to know they are contributing. I must communicate successes to my staff, just as I do with my volunteers. I let them know I couldn't do it without them. I show them how they contribute to organizational success and celebrate their individual achievements. I let them know how important they are to me.

And don't expect employees to be invested in our organizations unless we are invested in them. Study after study has shown that pay increases are *not* very motivating. We need to find out what is important to them. Listen and read between the lines. People want to feel they are doing something important, so let them know how important they are. Recognize and validate their contributions. They will reciprocate with good performance and heartfelt loyalty to us, our organizations, and our missions.

Staff Development

> Cultivate and support employees as you do volunteers.
>
> **Lessons Learned**

I give my staff the tools they need to improve their performance. They have working computers, as well as materials and supplies to train volunteers. They also receive continual training to maintain their skills. They are encouraged to take care of themselves and avoid burnout. I budget for computer supplies and maintenance, provide paid vacation, and allocate resources for both internal and external training.

Some things I can't provide through budgets and compensation packages. I want my employees to be productive, feel satisfied in their work, strive for excellence, work as a team, and take responsibility for their jobs. I want to empower them to reach their potential. This is the crux of staff development.

Providing structure and resources for your employees to succeed is part of the resource-based theory of human resource management.

observation

Enhancing Job Performance

I have found it best to treat my staff as if they want to do a good job. Most people want to succeed and feel good about themselves. Most often, people do poor work because a barrier is impeding them. Perhaps they weren't trained properly, misunderstood instructions, received unclear direction, were not given a deadline, or simply had too much to do.

We can control all these problems: write accurate job descriptions; provide up-to-date employee policies and procedures; implement a standard agency orientation; develop job-specific training programs; give employees an introductory period to learn their jobs; create a mentorship program; have new employees shadow more experienced staff. There are lots of things you can do to make sure employees know their jobs.

Enhancing Communication Skills

These job training methods work as well for volunteers as staff.

Lessons Learned

We must train our staff to be good communicators. To be good communicators, we must use the feedback loop, in which a listener feeds back what they just heard to the messenger. This gives both listener and messenger the opportunity to clarify the message. (For a more detailed discussion of the feedback loop, see my book *Power Your Organization's Fundraising: How the Partnership Paradigm Will Change Everything*.)

I also create a culture where it is safe to question—not to be insubordinate, but to question. This helps people use the feedback loop. If deadlines are not given or priorities are unclear, staff has permission to ask for clarification. In a culture of open communication, employees feel safe to ask about competing priorities, describe more effective or efficient approaches, and tell me when they won't be able to complete an assignment on time. I foster a culture of inquisitiveness and exploration. As a result, my employees pursue knowledge, contribute ideas, take risks, and implement innovative solutions.

Encouraging Personal Responsibility

When they are personally vested in the outcome, employees take greater pride in their work, gain satisfaction in completing difficult tasks, and take responsibility for each outcome. The trick is getting them personally vested. Luckily, there are many ways to accomplish these using internal and external motivators.

> A feedback loop is a communication mechanism that allows a sender and receiver to adjust their messages based on the difference between what was said and what was understood.
>
> definition

External Motivators

One external motivator is linking raises and bonuses to performance, i.e., give merit bonuses rather than cost of living increases. You can also tie raises to the organization's financial success. When the agency does well, some of the proceeds are distributed to employees. Or, you can combine the two. These motivators are used regularly in the for-profit world.

Another external motivator is praise. Not just general "good job" praise but specific praise for a specific accomplishment. For example, "Thank you for all your research on vendor costs. You saved me a lot of time, which freed me up to work on other tasks. And your research helped me negotiate a new vendor contract that saved us 20 percent over last year."

Specific praise tells an employee you are aware of their actions, appreciate their good work and that they made a valuable contribution to the agency's mission—which is why they work there in the first place.

> Research has shown that praise changes behavior. If you give specific praise, the action being praised will probably be repeated.
>
> important

Internal Motivators

One way to motivate employees is to give them goals without specifying how they should reach them. Let them figure it out and tell you what works best, then monitor progress based on their innovations. Your staff feels they have something to contribute and become vested in the process. Make the goals as specific as possible. To do this, you must have a goal-oriented mindset, be a good communicator and be willing to give up some control.

Let employees define their individual goals to help meet departmental and organizational goals. Let them define how they fit into the bigger picture and can best contribute. Again, you must have a strong, consistent vision, be willing to share your goals, create a culture that encourages healthy discussion, and give up even more control. Now you have a shared-leadership model.

Working with Individual Strengths and Weaknesses

> Using the shared-leadership model, I get highly productive, motivated staff working towards the same goals. I give up control over the details but improve the end product. It's a good trade.
>
> **Lessons Learned**

For-profits invest a lot of money into increasing productivity, improving quality, and boosting employee satisfaction. They know these investments will pay big dividends. Nonprofits can take advantage of the same tools to better leverage their resources, increase client satisfaction, and decrease employee turnover.

The Myers-Briggs Type Indicator

One of the most widely used tools to help people understand their work styles and preferences is the Myers-Briggs Type Indicator. Myers-Briggs is a personality inventory used by college and career counselors, executive coaches, and organizational consultants. It uses a psychometric questionnaire to measure psychological preferences: how people perceive the world.

Myers-Briggs groups people based on four categories: introversion/extroversion, sensing/intuitive, thinking/feeling, and judging/perceiving. These categories can be combined into sixteen different personality profiles. Individual differences within each profile can be measured through relative strengths in each category. Your particular combination indicates how you prefer to interact with others, solve problems, communicate, and make decisions. Myers-Briggs can help you figure out which tasks you most enjoy, how you prefer to accomplish them and the environment that best suits your work style.

I test right in the middle of the introversion/extroversion poles. This means I can find job satisfaction when working alone or working with other people. While planning my days, I try to schedule both solitary and group tasks. As a result, I get less frustrated than when I am working alone or in meetings all day.

Lessons Learned

Knowing which groupings your employees fall into will help everyone structure their assignments and work environment. Employees will feel more like giving their all in a less stressful environment.

For more information on the Myers-Briggs Type inventory, visit the Myers-Briggs Foundation website at www.myersbriggs.org.

The Highlands Ability Battery

Studies have shown that when employees maximize their natural abilities, they are more productive, less frustrated, make fewer mistakes, and have higher job satisfaction. Abilities are distinct from skills, which are developed from experience over time. Abilities are innate and remain constant over a lifetime. To uncover an employee's natural abilities, I highly recommend The Highlands Ability Battery.

I test low in attention to detail, which means I would not enjoy being an accountant or chemist. However, my low attention to detail means I see the big picture, which helps me define and communicate organizational vision.

Lessons Learned

Highlands is a series of work samples that measure natural abilities. How easily a participant completes a work sample indicates their underlying aptitude. Highlands tests for nineteen different natural abilities.

Results are matched with jobs each participant will find most fulfilling, providing an individualized abilities assessment. There is no right or wrong. In fact, there is strength in having a weak ability. The point is to learn how to best use your natural abilities.

The feedback I received on nineteen abilities guides my decisions on which tasks I should complete and which ones I should delegate. It also helps me understand how I perceive communications and which educational opportunities I should pursue.

For more information about The Highlands Ability Battery, visit http://highlandsco.com.

The DISC Assessment

Unlike Myers-Briggs, which measures personality preferences, or Highlands, which indicates natural abilities, the DISC (Dominance, Inducement, Submission, Compliance) Assessment measures individual behavior. Developed by John Geier, DISC is a group of psychological inventories that examines individuals in their normal environments.

> My DISC Assessment showed high driving behaviors. I get down to business quickly and get things done. I am more concerned with the external environment than the internal. I like challenges and thrive on solving complex problems. I work until the task is completed. To be most fulfilled, I need a job where these behaviors are welcomed.
>
> **Lessons Learned**

DISC groups behaviors into four quadrants: driving, influencing, steady, and compliant. The assessment tells you which roles are most comfortable, as well as how you function in specific work environments. Like Myers-Briggs, DISC results are self-reported. As with Highlands, both high and low scores indicate strengths and weaknesses. There is no right or wrong.

Knowing which behaviors employees engage in, and what they need from you, improves communication, helps you understand their work styles, decreases workplace conflict, and increases productivity.

For more information about the DISC Assessment, visit www.discprofile.com.

Encouraging Teamwork

Unless there is just one of you, which is impossible in a nonprofit, organizational objectives are accomplished through teams. As a result, team building is crucial.

> Creating a culture of teamwork and shared leadership motivates employees to be proactive and open and pursue excellence.
>
> **food for thought**

Many individual development techniques also work for team development. For example, defining and sharing roles and responsibilities tells individuals what they do, and lets their colleagues know how different roles fit together as a cohesive whole. It helps team members understand and accept different roles and perspectives and can improve communication.

Tying individual salary increases or bonuses to team accomplishments reinforces the importance of teamwork. In addition to individual goals, you can create team goals and can measure progress in both. You can structure employees' evaluations to measure their ability to complete tasks, work with others, and contribute to team success. This gives you the opportunity to praise both individual and team accomplishments.

Just as you would with individuals, let departments and work teams define their own ways to meet organizational goals. However, be aware of group dynamics, which can help or hinder individual contributions and reduce the team's ability to explore ideas. Make sure everyone is seen as an equal, integral part of the team, has opportunities to contribute, and all contributions are valued.

> I am particularly proud of three accomplishments I made during my first year: helping my director of programs excel in her new position; creating a cohesive team; and adding new staff in an orderly fashion.
>
> **stories from the real world**

In addition to individual testing and feedback, Myers-Briggs, Highlands, and DISC have team applications. If you can, take advantage of them. Using these tools can improve individual, team, and organizational performance.

> An executive director leads by example: whatever you do as the leader, your organization will replicate.
>
> **food for thought**

Leading by Example

As executive director, I lead by example. If I want my employees to work until they get the job done, I also stay late. If I want them to be on call for volunteers, I must be on call for employees. If I want them to be respectful to each other, I must respect each of them. If I want them to trust me, I must trust them.

Be consistent. Give both paid and unpaid staff job descriptions, agency orientations and adequate training. After telling your staff how they can contribute, validate their contributions. Train staff to communicate well. Invest in your employees. Give specific praise. Articulate organizational goals, then let employees define their own departmental, team and individual approaches. Capitalize on individual and team personality characteristics, abilities, and behaviors. Finally, don't expect your employees to do anything you don't model.

To Recap

- Articulate clear individual and team roles and responsibilities.
- Value and cultivate both paid and unpaid staff. Remember, monetary motivators are weak.
- Provide an optimal work structure for employees to perform effectively.
- Train your employees in good communication skills and foster a culture of open communication.
- Use both internal and external motivators to encourage personal responsibility.
- Identify and leverage individual and group strengths.
- Lead by example.

Chapter Nine

Working with the Community

IN THIS CHAPTER

- Meeting community needs
- Working with the community
- Interagency collaborations
- Mobilizing the community

Just as we can't implement organizational objectives on our own, our organizations can't implement their visions and missions alone. While individuals need help from organizational teams—board, staff, and volunteers—the organization needs help from other nonprofits and community partners. Our agency's vision tells the world what we hope to achieve. No matter how focused our missions, or small our target groups, we must partner with other organizations to succeed. Teamwork must extend beyond organizational walls into the community.

Meeting Community Needs

Your mission is not about your organization, it's about meeting community needs. No matter how broadly or narrowly you define it, your agency exists to serve that community. They don't care how big you are or how well you function internally, they care about your ability to meet their needs. As executive director, you must maintain your organization's focus on this resounding truth. To the broader community, organizational operations don't matter at all. It's the product that counts.

First, you need to be relevant. What you accomplish must matter to the people you serve. This is why it's important to base your funding appeals on community needs. Relevance begins with information. It's not enough to say you're doing good work. You need to back up those statements with either your own research or data from other authorities. A thorough community needs assessment is the first step to being relevant.

To be relevant, people need to know you exist. This is where public relations and communications come into play. By communicating your mission, people learn who you are and get involved. Your marketing and public relations strategies are not about helping your organization, but rather about helping the community. All of your communications should focus on community needs and how well you meet them.

> Community data can be found at your local United Way, government agencies, and community foundations.
>
> practical tip

The community also wants you to use public and individual resources wisely. People who have benefitted from these resources want them in place for someone else. This could be true for a variety of issues: health, pets, education, the arts. Meeting community needs is part of your donor acquisition and retention strategy. Again, resource development is not about raising money, it is about meeting community needs.

Hopefully, your agency represents a wise use of public money, generating immediate benefits or preventing long-term problems. You may achieve your goals using fewer resources and show a tremendous return on investment. As a result, your financial management strategy is, once again, about mission.

In fact, everything your agency does is about your capacity to meet community needs.

Working with the Community

Nonprofits exist to meet community needs, are governed by community members, and are supported by community contributions. A nonprofit's tax exempt and legal status means its proceeds must be reinvested in its mission, making it ultimately accountable to the community.

Do you understand your community's needs? Does your communications strategy focus on them? What about your resource development plan? How wisely do you use public resources? Do you keep community needs in mind when creating your financial management strategy?

food for thought

For most executive directors—caught up in day-to-day operations, dealing with major donors, keeping the board happy, motivating staff, worrying about finances, and addressing crises—it's not easy to even think about their duty to the public. However, it's crucial to find the time and energy to carry out community-focused responsibilities.

You must be part of the community and work to improve it. To accomplish this, you work with other community agencies—nonprofit, for-profit, and governmental—in a cooperative spirit.

My organization does not receive any government funding, nor am I a member of our local Human Services Advisory Council, a government committee that discusses funding issues and their impact on human services. With no government funding, it's not important for me to be part of this committee's work. Yet, I make it a priority to attend its meetings. I want to know who the other nonprofit human services players are, what community needs they are meeting, and how I might collaborate with them. As a result, I increase the council's awareness of my organization, our reputation and our credibility with the public, while better serving the community.

We also partner with a local gas company. This collaboration is designed to build relationships, rather than raise money. The company works with the local high school system, conducting a mentorship program and working with youth as part of their community service. They have already figured out the school system's politics and how to get things done, are well known in the community, and put a lot of resources into public relations.

By partnering with the gas company, we meet the community's needs more efficiently. The company provides a gateway into the schools. As we partner, their credibility rubs off on us. My funders love it, as it leverages their contributions to meet a defined community need.

Interagency Collaborations

Your mission is bigger than your organization. Your community has enormous needs—more than one organization can handle. You need partners to help you do the job. It's important to know your community and who will make a good partner.

> **T**ogether
>
> **E**veryone
>
> **A**ccomplishes
>
> **M**ore
>
> **food for thought**

Organizations with Similar Missions

To find natural partners, seek out organizations with similar missions. They may work in a different community, another age group, or a different income bracket, but their services are comparable to yours. These partnerships are natural, as you both do pretty much the same thing. You might partner to advocate for certain legislation, provide shared employee trainings, or apply for funding. Because you have similar missions, your organizations will share commonalities and can accomplish much together to benefit the community.

With scarce resources, funding agencies are looking for collaborations between like organizations to reduce duplicative services.

Organizations with Complementary Missions

Organizations with complementary missions don't do what you do, but partnering with them benefits your respective constituencies. For example, a crisis hotline partners with a counseling center or police department. Or an agency that provides housing for people with disabilities partners with a service provider with a similar clientele. Referral relationships and service agreements are common. Shared events, such as conferences or fundraisers, can attract the same audience and benefit all partners.

> In my community, there are several service providers for people with developmental disabilities. They all need their staffs trained to address varying issues. The largest agency opened its standard employee trainings to the others, a win-win. The large agency met its training objectives, while the smaller organizations trained their staffs more economically.
>
> **stories from the real world**

Conferences are a great way to provide information and perspectives for participants, build relationships with other agencies and show interagency collaboration.

Partnerships between complementary agencies, or those with similar clients, can often take the same form. For example, advocating for legislation that benefits overlapping client groups or partnering to form a fundraising collaborative.

> Information and referral relationships are among the easiest ways to show broad community involvement and fulfill the mission. Whether the relationship is formal or informal, document these relationships, particularly in funding applications.
>
> **practical tip**

Organizations with Similar Needs

Organizations with similar needs can also form partnerships. All businesses need to lower overhead. Agencies can form buying collaboratives to reduce costs for office supplies, health insurance, or other goods and services. They might join professional or industry associations, like the Chamber of Commerce, Center for Nonprofits, Child Welfare League of America, or American Association of Suicidology, to share information. Or they might share staff, such as fundraisers or accountants. These collaborations free up resources to meet community needs.

Organizations with Similar Markets

Few people in nonprofits think in marketing terms. As a result, few agencies approach organizations with similar markets as potential partners. Most often, these market partnerships are between for-profits and nonprofits, creating employee volunteer programs, cause marketing relationships, and other collaborations.

> Often, membership packages for large business, nonprofit, and professional associations come with discounts for commonly used goods and services.
>
> **food for thought**

One of the biggest differences between nonprofits and for-profits is the variety of markets nonprofits serve. Both offer goods and services to consumers. But at nonprofits, the people who pay for the services are usually different

Business interest in giving to nonprofits is a relatively recent phenomenon. The prevailing philosophy had been that business philanthropy actually hurt nonprofits and was bad for the community. During the early part of the twentieth century, businesses kept their corporate interests separate from philanthropic ones, feeling that mixing them diluted their effectiveness. How times change.

observation

from those who benefit from them. For example, government and foundations are big nonprofit funders. In addition, many nonprofits survive on volunteer labor and individual donations, making the public another important market.

As their name indicates, for-profits seek profit. They have products that appeal to certain people. They want their name to get out to as many potential consumers as possible. They also want to lower production costs, especially labor costs. What reduces these costs? Giving back to the community and making the world a better place translates into increased employee loyalty and productivity, reducing turnover, lowering unit costs and enhancing quality. What business doesn't want that?

Partnering with a nonprofit is an easy way for businesses to give back to the community. For-profits form their own foundations and encourage employee volunteerism, match their employees' gifts, and give a percentage of their sales to a cause. As a result, employees become more attached to their community.

Nonprofit leaders need to know their markets and where they intersect with a for-profit's. Is the nonprofit's consumer base the same as the for-profit's? Does the for-profit want to get its products in front of your consumers? Your employees? Your donors?

Event sponsorships are a tried and true way for corporations to get their names in front of your consumers and donors.

practical tip

Do you have access to government, specifically legislators? Who do you invite to your special events? How can a for-profit become involved with your mission *and* meet the people who make the laws?

There are many ways for your nonprofit to partner with organizations with similar markets.

Mobilizing the Community

Executive directors are more than leaders in their own organizations; they are also leaders in the community. You must mobilize your board, staff, volunteers, and your community.

Mobilizing a community begins with a communications strategy. You exist to meet a community need. Therefore, you must create awareness of that need by putting the issue in front of the public. Create and implement a communications strategy using: press releases, speaking engagements, advertising, journal or magazine articles, letters to the editor, newsletters, annual reports, emails, Facebook posts, or tweets. Whichever vehicles you choose, stay focused on your issues.

> People want to make significant, meaningful contributions. Do you have mechanisms in place to let them?
>
> **food for thought**

You also need to give people ways to get involved. Let them know how they can give back to their community. If you are asking for financial support, relate giving opportunities to community needs. (We talked about resource development in **Chapter Seven**.) Provide your donors the opportunity to give significantly. What kind of fundraising strategy do you have? What is your emphasis? Are you giving people ways to give all they can?

On a nonfinancial level, what volunteer opportunities do you offer? Are they significant and meaningful? How do you let people know about these opportunities? Do you partner with your local United Way to advertise them? How about corporations? Do you reward your volunteers for a job well done? (We talked about working with volunteers in the last chapter.)

> Does your organization's structure support meeting the community's needs?
>
> **food for thought**

You also have to respond to legislation that impacts your mission. If meeting your organization's community need is important to your stakeholders, you must let them know when their interests are at risk. Know what's happening around you and share it with others. Create a communications strategy to disseminate information quickly. Give people ways to take action. Get them involved in the processes that affect their lives. In other words, be an effective advocate for your cause.

Meeting your mission goes well beyond your organization. To meet community needs, you must be accountable to the community around you. For maximum impact, partner with other community organizations, be they for-profits, other nonprofits, or government agencies. You can collaborate with other nonprofits based on mission, need or target market. Mobilize your community, making sure you are giving people the opportunity to give back at the level they feel most fulfilled. Embrace your role as a community leader.

To Recap

- Meet community needs through wise resource allocation.
- For the most impact, partner with other community agencies: nonprofit, for-profit, and governmental.
- Develop collaborations with organizations with similar missions, complementary missions, similar needs, and similar markets.
- Be a leader in your community as well as your organization.

Chapter Ten

Building for the Future

IN THIS CHAPTER

- Planning to plan
- Laying the operational foundation
- Laying the financial foundation
- Playing off my base motivators
- Growth Issues

Planning should begin as soon as you start the job. My first plans were short-term: things that needed to be done in the first three months. From there, I extended to annual and then long-term planning.

I came in October, and I knew my first priority was to get us through the end of the year. To start crafting a road map, I met with individual board members. To enhance revenue, I worked hard on the gala and the holiday appeal. In addition, I had board meetings and the following year's budget and was already looking beyond the short-term.

Board feedback, along with the budgeting process, helped me focus on what I needed to accomplish with board, staff, and volunteers to promote our mission. I figured out the types of revenue I had to generate. I also needed to enhance community awareness, and I knew which groups would best help me get there.

Planning to Plan

I had lots of questions to answer. What did I want the organization to look like in the long-term? How would the board and I interpret and fulfill our mission? What kind of staffing structure would best support our goals? Which revenue structure made the most sense? What were our opportunities, and were we in a position to take advantage of them? What were our threats, and how could we manage them?

These questions are part of the strategic planning process. Since my agency was in crisis, we didn't even start asking them until nine months into my tenure.

> I was happy it only took us nine months to start strategic planning. The board could now concentrate on long-term vision, rather than day-to-day crisis management. I was pleased we had gotten this far in less than a year.
>
> **stories from the real world**

But strategic planning takes time. First, we formed focus groups to research the larger environment. At this moment, these groups have not yet reported their results. We are still in the early stages.

We made several changes before the formal strategic planning process. For example, we updated the mission statement to reflect our ability to utilize a variety of communication platforms, not just telephones. The board and I revised the mission statement together before voting on it.

We also needed a values statement, and I asked the board president to work with me to define one. We have yet to discuss it as a full board, but we have a starting point.

Strategic planning is like flying a plane and charting a course at the same time. We had to move forward without knowing our destination. I needed agreement on mission and values to succeed in the short-term. As for the rest, our organizational and environmental assessments would have to do.

To get us through the year it would take to formulate a strategic plan, we outlined what we needed to succeed without one.

Laying the Operational Foundation

We had all the ingredients for success. My program implementation experience was helpful. The agency had a long-time training director (who became my director of programs), and we had our listener training down pat. In addition, we had a highly dedicated volunteer base, along with the necessary certifications to validate our quality standards.

Program-wise, we were in good shape. I wanted to continue our tradition of excellence, and I knew the board agreed. So, I wasn't going to tinker much with our training or volunteer structure.

Volunteers are the lifeblood of our organization. Recruitment and retention are primary concerns for staff, board, and volunteer leaders. We wanted to continue to support our volunteers, while exercising budgetary prudence.

> God bless my predecessors, who had the foresight to build and implement a strong training and volunteer structure.
>
> **stories from the real world**

With a paid staff of three, I had to restructure clerical support. When my administrative support person began looking for another job, I decided not to replace her. Also, in addition to a training expert, we needed volunteer management leadership. We had more than a hundred volunteers; they deserved a staff person dedicated to their needs.

I brought development expertise. At least temporarily, I would implement agency fundraising activities, except special events. I hired a special event planner. To generate community awareness and support, I hired a public relations consultant. In addition, I brought in a freelance web developer to bolster our online presence and a bookkeeper for internal controls and audits.

I was the only full-time exempt staff. The director of programs and the volunteer manager were part-time exempt and the rest were independent contractors.

The job descriptions were revised to reflect our individual and team strengths and weaknesses. As we added staff, we hired skilled, experienced people, who fit into our culture, augmented our strengths, and complemented our weaknesses.

This staff structure provided the highest quality operational support at the most economical cost. It also laid a good foundation for growth, as we knew we would be adding volunteers and staff.

Laying the Financial Foundation

Laying the financial structure, per se, was not that difficult. I mean, a budget is a budget. (For more on budgeting, see my book *Succeed in Your Nonprofit Funding Partnerships: Analyzing Their Costs and Benefits*.) If all we needed were budgets, we would be in good shape. However, we would need more to prepare for the funding structure after strategic planning.

As a former development director, I knew we would need airtight policies and procedures to compete for government funding. They would have to govern conflicts of interest, grievances, drugs and alcohol, smoking, nondiscrimination, and harassment. While we might not need all these for every application, each one might be required by some agency, at some point. My philosophy was be prepared. Plus, it didn't hurt to have them; in fact, it brought needed structure. So, revising the employee manual was one of my first tasks.

I am also experienced at creating corporate partnerships. To garner corporate support, I would need marketing materials business people could relate to. For example, companies are interested in who's at the helm, so I needed a public relations document about me: background, achievements, and vision. Since I don't promote myself well, my public relations consultant came in handy.

> With the exception of job searches, I generally don't do well at self-promotion. Plus, I need distance to see myself clearly. I have learned to get outside perspectives.
>
> **Lessons Learned**

I also needed a piece about our organization: who we were, how we operated, and the benefits we could provide a business and the community it serves. Again, a consultant's job.

And finally, I needed a piece about our finances: a one-page, easy-to-understand document with charts and graphs. I created pie charts showing where our money came from and where it went. I built a bar graph showing our financial growth (Examples of charts are shown in **Chapter Six**).

Now I was equipped to go after short-term funding. And, if we decided to change or add to our existing revenue structure, I had laid the foundation for additional materials.

For more information on what governmental, corporate, and foundation contributors look for, see my book *Confessions of a Successful Grants Writer: A Complete Guide to Discovering and Obtaining Funding.*

Playing Off My Base Motivators

My DISC assessment showed both my work style and my base motivators. For example, I am a very social person and highly motivated by relationships. I love relationship building, as you can probably tell from my emphasis on team building. My number one motivator is being able to build and strengthen satisfying, productive relationships. One reason I am happy at my job is my complete immersion in relationship building with staff, board, volunteers, vendors, funders, and community partners. My business is based on relationships, which is fortunate since that's the way I work.

When I became an executive director, I had to come to terms with power and control. I knew I had power and control, I just didn't know how I was going to use them. I needed to define a leadership style that was going to work for me and the organization.

One of my motivators is economic utility. I am frugal and understand the importance of money. I value getting the most bang for my buck, but I don't negotiate based on money, which is just a commodity to pursue mission. Relationships are my primary motivator.

Why did I find this important for planning? I had to create structures that worked best for me and the agency. My staff needed to understand what was important to me. My board interactions had to be comfortable for all concerned. I had to understand how I interpreted the world around me.

Everyone has different motivators, so I know to ask questions and get clarification. Because I understand my own strengths and weaknesses, I get other people's input. Knowing how I am motivated gives me a guidepost to move forward.

Understanding my own style and values, and being able to articulate them, helps me be consistent in my words and actions. It helps me be authentic, transparent, and build trust.

Know your prime motivators and define your leadership style. Share them with others. Live them. Build trust.

food for thought

Trust is what I need to move forward. By giving away power through relationships, I actually gain it back. People trust me and are willing to follow my lead. Understanding my base motivators, letting others know how I will achieve a goal and following through make all the difference.

Issues with Growth

To expand our mission, we need to grow. Growth is generally a good thing. More staff and volunteers mean more work gets done. More money generally means more financial stability. Gaining expertise increases credibility. Growing relationships means more trust.

But growth is not always good. In the short-term, you may have to expend resources before realizing revenues, causing a cash flow crisis. For example, you may need to hire staff to implement a program that realizes revenue through reimbursement. You might need more office space, generating expansion and/or moving costs. You might need to add staff to market a new service. Whatever the reason, when you grow, you will probably experience some sort of short-term cash crunch.

In the short term, before you can hire staff or get a new building, your current staff and facilities will be stretched to their limits. The staff might be overworked and experience fatigue and stress, which generally means more mistakes and less productivity. Morale might go down, as people's needs go unmet for lack of resources. Interpersonal relationships might be stressed, damaging the workplace environment.

Growth also brings change and, with it, uncertainty. People fear the unknown. They don't know how things will be. They wonder what's going to happen to them. Most people prefer the ebb and flow of familiarity.

None of this is reason not to grow. There are always solutions. You can plan on using cash reserves, or taking out a line of credit, to cover short-term cash flow issues. You can implement extra staff appreciation activities to bolster morale. You can prepare people for what's coming. As you grow, be prepared for the negatives, as well as the positives.

> Growth means change and change is stressful, even if it is perceived positively. If you are planning to grow, plan to deal with organizational stress.
>
> **Lessons Learned**

Planning for the future is a daunting but manageable task. As you take on the executive director role, you will engage in short-term, annual and long-term planning. You can lay the basic organizational and financial structure to anticipate future plans. Knowing your primary motivators helps you define your leadership style; sharing that style with others helps build trust. Growth can be good and bad—be prepared.

To Recap

- Embrace planning for the future.
- Make sure you have a strong organizational foundation to accomplish your goals.
- Prepare materials that will support your financial structure.
- Know your primary motivators and leadership style.
- Be ready for the good and bad consequences of growth.

Chapter Eleven

Personal Development

IN THIS CHAPTER

- Knowing and articulating my values
- The importance of self-awareness
- Being confident
- The road to personal development

An organization's health is a reflection of its leadership. If leadership is solid, organizations tend to do well. If it's poor, they unravel. Of course, an agency's health is affected by other factors too, some beyond a leader's control, such as the economic climate. But how well an organization takes advantage of opportunities and deals with threats is a direct reflection on its leadership.

What prepared me most for this aspect of leadership? Personal development.

Knowing and Articulating My Values

Leaders create corporate culture.

Corporate culture largely determines how decisions are made. It defines corporate ethics, i.e., what is acceptable; tells board, staff, and volunteers which risks are worth taking; and lets everyone know which behaviors will be tolerated. In short, corporate culture determines organizational life, as well as how, and how successfully, mission is achieved. Since fulfilling your mission is the ultimate measure of organizational success, a healthy corporate culture is imperative. As keeper of the corporate culture, defining, articulating, and implementing values is one of the executive director's most important roles.

> Culture is the aggregation of behaviors, values, beliefs, and characteristics of a particular social, ethnic, or age group.
>
> Corporate culture is the aggregated behaviors, values, beliefs, and characteristics of a corporation or organization.
>
> definition

Defining values starts at the personal level. Knowing your personal values helps you determine which work environment is the best fit. In the search for an executive director, organizational and executive values must align. If not, there will be major problems with the board, the other keepers of organizational values. Starting off in conflict with the board is a bad idea. To avoid this, you must understand your own personal values.

Keep in mind, the organization's culture may not be its healthiest when you get there. If you are hired as a change agent, part of your job will be to fix the corporate culture. But you better make sure that the values you want to implement are the same ones your board wants. Otherwise, the conflict will rock the organization until the board is replaced or resigns, or the board replaces you. None of these outcomes are good for you or the organization, which could take years to recover. In short, know your values and how well they align with the board's before you accept the job.

If you are hired to change the culture, as I was, knowing and articulating your values is especially important. The first step is understanding what you want the culture to be. Then, you can assess what the culture is at that moment and implement policies and procedures that reinforce the values you want to keep and uphold the ones you want to introduce. To manage that shift, you must articulate values so people know where they are headed and can decide whether they want to go there. If they don't share your values, they will leave. They'll kick and scream first, but when you stick to your guns, they will either adjust or leave. That is part of managing change.

Even if you are not hired to change the culture, you *will* change it simply by exerting leadership. Here's where understanding your operating principles will help. The organization will live your values. The agency can only be as ethical as you are. How consistently you live your stated values tells others what they can expect from you. As the executive, you will need a guide for making decisions, especially among competing priorities. Knowing and articulating your values helps your board, staff, and volunteers understand your decisions, which helps them feel grounded during turmoil.

> It's not uncommon for people to leave an organization after executive transitions. They might leave at any level: board, staff, or volunteer. I lost two board members, out of ten, within three months of starting.
>
> **Lessons Learned**

Understanding your own values also helps you face tough decisions or endure flak for ones you have already made. Knowing that you did the right thing, even when it was unpopular, helps you get through criticism.

The Importance of Self-Awareness

One of my greatest strengths is self-awareness. Understanding my strengths and weaknesses, abilities, preferences, and communication style has served me well, especially as an executive director.

For example, I know that I am an auditory learner. Although I have other learning channels, listening is my strongest. My second strongest is movement. My weakest is reading. So, when I need to really know something, I have conversations with people and write down the important points. I do well with workshops, seminars, webinars, meetings, and phone conversations.

> According to The Highlands Abilities Battery, there are five main learning channels: reading, hearing, movement, design, and number. Reading and hearing are the main formal education channels. Often, people aren't even aware of the other channels.
>
> **observation**

I do not do well with pure written communication: books, letters, emails, and texts. When I read books, it takes me a long time because I outline them. When I get a letter, I read and re-read to make sure I understand its content. If instructions are included, I usually call the sender to clarify them. It's a running joke between me and my board president that when we talk on the phone, sweet music results; when we email, we get frustrated. Oral communication is my key to success.

Also, I am a big picture person. I can see how systems work and how smaller pieces fit together as part of the whole. I do well setting objectives. I enjoy creating a vision and planning methods to achieve that vision. I like identifying and developing strategic relationships and take pleasure in developing my staff. I am very good at these tasks, which serve me well in my leadership role.

However, I am terrible at details. For example, I am not a good proofreader. I make mistakes on financial spreadsheets and miss fine print in contracts. I get impatient with tedious, thorough, and methodical tasks, which are not great traits for an executive director.

So what do I do? I rely on others to compensate for my weaknesses. Just like my strengths, I have chosen to accept my weaknesses for what they are. Rather than spending all my time and effort going against my grain, I play off my strengths and compensate for my weaknesses. People want to contribute to the mission, so I let them help.

After nine months, I finally figured out how to create accurate financials for my board and understand how those figures were derived.

1. I create the first draft of the financial reports.
2. I send my draft to the treasurer, who reviews it and, invariably, finds mistakes.
3. My treasurer makes revisions, sends it back to me and follows up with a phone call.
4. To help me learn, he patiently tells me what revisions he has made and why.
5. We continue this process until we have accurate spreadsheets.

I am lucky. My treasurer is thorough, methodical, and comprehensive. He is also patient and takes a lot of time to help me out.

Lessons Learned

I rely on the board treasurer to review my financial projections; the board attorney to review contracts; and the director of programs to make sure I have included all operational details in grants. If details are involved, I have someone else review my work. They want to help, all I do is let them.

My treasurer is not the only board member who has helped me. One member helped me with technology. Another, a retired businessman, helped me create marketing position statements, identify target markets, and develop products to meet market needs. One board member was also a volunteer listener. She helped me understand how my ideas impacted the front lines. Everyone on my board has contributed something, because I knew what to ask for and how they could help.

Being Confident

As a leader, you must have confidence in your abilities, perceptions, and decisions. If you feel good about who you are and have confidence in yourself, it shows in your leadership. As an executive director, you will be asked to tackle challenges that are new to you and the organization. If you lead them down a road they haven't been before, or risk resources to accomplish something that has never been done, you better exude confidence. Other people will be doubtful and will need to see your confidence and know that you have things under control.

You must also have a strong ego to handle criticism. "You can't please all of the people all of the time." Someone will always disagree with your decisions or how you implement them.

As executive director you have a broader perspective than anyone else in the organization. There will be times when your staff or volunteers do not understand a decision and you cannot share all the facts with them. They might vehemently disagree with you and grumble to others, who also don't have the facts. You could face a lot of criticism from a lot of people. Don't let these attitudes rock you.

You must be confident enough to ask for help. Healthy self-esteem and confidence does *not* mean you have to go it alone. However, it does mean you know what you can and cannot do and when you need help. Being able to reach out to others is a measure of strength. You will not have all the answers. In fact, you will not always know the right questions to ask.

You have a staff to help carry out day-to-day operations. Use them. They want the organization to succeed to grow in their jobs. You have a board to help you plan and set vision. The board is vested in organizational success—they have legal and fiduciary responsibilities. You have consultants who want business and good references. And, you have people who willingly give their time, treasure, or talent to make sure you succeed. You have lots of support. Let people contribute.

> If you are a people pleaser and want everyone to be happy with you all the time, executive leadership is not for you. If you don't like conflict, value peace at all costs, executive leadership is not for you.
>
> **Lessons Learned**

People with healthy self-esteem defend their opinions, even when faced with opposition, but are secure enough to modify them when given new information. These people trust their own judgment and do not feel guilty when others don't like their choices. They live in the present, don't worry excessively about the past, and trust in their abilities to solve problems. Confident people ask for help when they need it and consider themselves equal to others, accepting differences in abilities, perspectives, prestige, or finances. They are sensitive to others' needs, accept normal rules of behavior, and don't look to prosper at anyone else's expense.

People with poor self-esteem are dissatisfied with who they are. They might engage in heavy self-criticism, as well as being hypersensitive to criticism from others. They feel attacked, resenting anyone who points out their flaws, can live in a state of chronic indecision, and have exaggerated fears of making a mistake. Some might want to please others at all costs. Others are perfectionists and show frustration when it is not achieved. They might dwell on past mistakes or exhibit hostility for no apparent reason. Or, they could be pessimists, always looking for the worst in people or situations.

> Self-esteem is a person's sense of self-worth, stemming from their perceptions of their own value and capabilities.
>
> **definition**

Obviously, a person with strong self-esteem is better equipped to lead. Anything you can do to develop and maintain healthy self-esteem is worth the investment.

With a healthier self-view, you will exude the necessary confidence to be an effective leader.

The Road to Personal Development

I am fortunate. I have the resources to explore personal development.

Education has been invaluable. The investments I have made in continuing education have helped me tremendously. Both my formal and professional educational experiences have expanded my knowledge base and skills, making me be a better employee and leader.

Career testing has helped me understand myself. Meyers-Briggs, Highlands, and DISC have provided insights into who I am, my natural strengths and how to leverage my abilities to achieve maximum satisfaction and effectiveness. (We talked about these tools in **Chapter Eight**.)

Taking this information and working with a career consultant and an executive coach have helped me manage interpersonal communications and work with others as part of a team. These team building insights have allowed me to shape and define organizational roles and develop staff and volunteers.

Counseling has helped me understand how I interpret the world, the reasons behind my behaviors, to be aware of my feelings, and what to do once I understand them. Counseling has helped me become self-aware.

Your road to personal development might be different. When I went to school, there were no formal studies in nonprofit management, philanthropy, or fundraising. Now they abound. There are also many books, professional seminars, and workshops that were not available early in my career. Don't neglect your personal development. It will be one of the best investments you ever make.

Understanding your personal values helps you shape corporate culture. Increasing your self-awareness helps you know when to ask for help. Showing confidence is important to move the organization forward. Find your road to personal development. The investment is worth it.

To Recap

- Define and articulate your values.
- Improve your self-awareness.
- Have confidence in your abilities, perceptions, and decisions.
- Pursue personal development.

Chapter Twelve

Work/Life Balance

IN THIS CHAPTER

- Scheduling personal time
- Engaging in self-care activities
- Tapping into personal support systems

Like most of my colleagues, work/life balance is a big challenge. Accepting an executive director position with an organization is like getting married, as we talked about in **Chapter Two**. Being in a committed, all-encompassing personal relationship, as well as an all-encompassing professional one, is tough on personal and family life. Work/life issues abound, and you will get caught in the middle.

Scheduling Personal Time

I had to come to terms with time management. Don't get me wrong, I can handle multiple tasks with tight deadlines. I don't have a problem doing my job. The problem is I love my job too much. I get along well with my board, like my colleagues, and enjoy the work. Sometimes, I get so caught up in a task, I lose track of time. In other words, I'm a workaholic, a common malady among executives.

Although working relentlessly produces great short-term gains, the long-term results aren't as satisfying. We get weary; the job becomes a chore; and other relationships suffer from inattention. If we're not careful, we burn out. To fight it, I take time away from the job. This helps maintain my enthusiasm and some semblance of sanity.

Early in my career, I experienced job burnout. I took on so much work it was all I ever did. Superb job performance was my only focus. I soon lost enthusiasm for the job, became irritable at work and home, and ultimately couldn't function well personally and professionally. I needed a leave of absence.

I ended up quitting the job. Recognizing I had work/life boundaries to work on, I went into business for myself, worked part-time and determined my own workload. I also got into therapy (this was before executive coaches were popular).

I worked for myself for five years, until I got tired of my one-person organization, and found a better balance between my work and personal life.

Lessons Learned

When I became an executive director, I had difficulty adjusting to the demands on my time. I had to work evenings and weekends to meet with the board and other volunteers. Even now, I am out two or three nights a week and work two Saturdays each month.

At first, I thought losing personal and family time was just part of the transition. Eventually, I would learn to better manage the workload. Time would magically appear after I became more proficient in the new role. I was in denial. It took me six months to realize the job's all-encompassing nature wasn't going to change. If I didn't manage the demands, I was never going to have any personal or family time.

So, I went back to my strengths, especially planning and prioritizing. I have an innate ability to plan. I defined my values, worked off my strengths and set personal objectives with timeframes.

This meant scheduling time to attend family outings and address personal needs. I entered personal agenda items in my calendar as appointments. I instructed my executive coach to ask about

Be ready for major transitions when becoming executive director. The job can consume you.

food for thought

personal endeavors, making sure I scheduled them and followed through.

I needed an attitude change. Because my professional and personal lives were all-consuming, I needed to relax my reliance on stringent blocks of work time. For example, I learned it was okay to occasionally take a long lunch with a friend rather than working through or only having business lunches. If I had worked the evening before, I could take a morning to get my hair done. I functioned better if I scheduled time for me. As a result, my agency was better off.

What is measured is what gets done. I needed someone to measure my progress balancing work and personal life. Just like work objectives, I needed someone to hold me accountable for meeting personal objectives.

I still have qualms about using precious time for (what seems like) frivolous indulgence. However, I must remember my values. It's important that my agency function well. For that to happen, I must function well. So, taking care of me is important.

Lessons Learned

If I want my organization to be balanced, I need to be balanced. For employees to feel free to take care of themselves, I need to set the example. Taking care of the organization is important to me, so taking care of myself became a priority.

Engaging in Self-Care Activities

For whatever reasons, I have difficulty with self-care. I place a much higher priority on meeting other people's needs. I would sacrifice everything to make sure someone else was taken care of. It took me a long time to realize that some of my energy needed to be directed towards me. If I wasn't renewing my own emotional stash, I wouldn't have anything left to give.

Today, I am more balanced. True, I work two or three nights a week and still feel guilty about taking a long lunch. But it's better. I talked about celebrating organizational progress in **Chapter Two**. It's the same with personal progress.

As I have said, it took me six months to realize the all-encompassing nature of executive leadership. At that point, I began keeping a schedule of self-care activities.

> Self-care is personal emotional, mental, and physical health maintenance. A self-care activity is any individual action intended to restore health or prevent illness.
>
> definition

Self-care is taking time for personal comfort. It is everything you do to revitalize, escape the daily grind, forget the demands on your time, and relax. Self-care is different for everyone and critically important for an executive director.

I get my nails done every two weeks, my hair styled once a month, and pedicures about every six weeks. I don't bring my cell phone. Having people dote on me—massage my head, hands, or feet—provides a brief vacation from work stress. My caregivers aren't interested in what I do for a living. I have no goals or objectives to meet. People chit chat about nothing. And, without my cell phone, I get a real break. For me, this is self-care at its best. (If you are a man, you probably have different activities.) Regular self-care helps me function better.

One self-care activity is taking time off. Most of us go on vacation. If we're smart, we make ourselves less accessible. For me, this means setting up an emergency communication chain—instructing my colleagues to contact me only in an emergency.

> My director of programs teaches the importance of self-care to our volunteers. People on a crisis line definitely need time away. She is constantly commending me on my efforts.
>
> stories from the real world

With my new position, the length and frequency of my time off changed drastically. Before, I would take two-week vacations twice a year: during the summer and between Christmas and New Year's. But as an executive director, I didn't feel I could be gone that long. Plus, with the constant demands, I needed more frequent breaks. I changed my approach, going on two- or three-day jaunts every couple of months, plus a week in the summer and a week before New Year's. I didn't start off with that plan. It took me months to figure out what would work.

Tapping into Personal Support Systems

Know which activities relax you and make time for them. You need a break to reenergize. You are worth it.

food for thought

We are social beings. We need people who know and love us and accept us unconditionally. If you are a workaholic, you may try to get these needs met through your professional relationships. But work is not the best place to find friendship and intimacy. Work relationships are permeated by organizational priorities. If there is conflict between an organizational priority and a personal relationship, the organization generally comes first. It's a good idea to keep your personal life separate from your work life.

Unfortunately, many executive directors have a hard time creating this separation. With so many needs to be met, it's hard to find time for movies, dinner parties, community clubs, or any social outing.

But finding time for friends and family is crucial. Who else knows me and likes me unconditionally? They couldn't care less about my work, except how it affects my well-being. I have my to nurture relationships with people who have nothing to do with my job.

Just as I do with self-care, I schedule time to foster my friendships. The old adage, "All work and no play make Jack a dull boy," is true. Without friends, I will end my career with terrific professional accolades and absolutely no one to share them with. The accolades will fade; solid relationships will endure. It pays big dividends to give friends and family time and attention.

Numerous psychological studies have shown that people with more developed social and personal support systems fare better in difficult times.

food for thought

I'm not great at setting boundaries. I struggle constantly to balance work, personal, family, and friend time. That's why I work on it with my executive coach. (I talked about investing in an executive coach in **Chapter Two**.)

To effectively serve my organization and community, I must take care of my personal and social needs. I must schedule time for myself. I must engage in self-care and social activities. I must build my personal network as I do my professional ones. In other words, I must take care of my whole self. My organization and I are better off for it.

To Recap

- Schedule personal time as rigorously as you do work activities
- Build an accountability structure to meet personal goals, just as you do with professional goals
- Take time for self-care
- Build your personal network as you do your professional network

Conclusion

Wrapping It All Up

Becoming an executive director is a huge transition. To succeed, you must rely on your experiences, strengths, and expertise. In addition, you must learn new skills, engage in new behaviors, work well with other people, know your leadership style, and be aware of your strengths and weaknesses. Be honest. Nonprofit executive leadership requires a lot. It is an all-encompassing job.

Many executive directors find opportunities to learn more about budgeting and financial management, evaluation and outcome measures, resource development, and human resources. Learning these disciplines helped them in their new roles, no matter what their path to the big chair. These are skills you want to build up. Most importantly, know when you need help and take advantage when it's offered.

Start your new job with an arsenal of support. Create a short-term and annual plan, and then celebrate each small success with board, staff, and volunteers. Be prepared for some decisions to be unpopular. There will always be someone who disagrees with a decision or how you implemented it, especially in larger organizations. You are not alone—develop relationships with other executive directors. Sometimes, investing in professional support, like an executive coach, can help.

As you begin your transition, remember: you will experience a honeymoon and it will end. When that happens, accept the new friction as a sign of deepening relationships. Embrace the tension and use it to your advantage. Build on these relationships to lay a strong foundation.

Your relationship with the board is the key to success. Working with the board is your most important task. Be aware, your role with the board is fluid: boss, team player and employee. Develop a good relationship with the president, as this affects your relationship with the whole board. You now report to a group of people, instead of one supervisor. Recognize group dynamics and manage them carefully.

The job can be overwhelming and frenetic. Everything demands your attention all the time. You will need to create mechanisms to make work manageable. Prioritize you workload based on long- and short-term objectives. Consider internal and external constituencies. Work on communication skills and trust-building activities to delegate more effectively.

To implement your mission, you must manage money. Where you allocate your financial resources is a statement of organizational values. Managing expenses is often easier than managing revenues. You must also watch cash flow and prepare for months with negative net income. Understanding return on investment and profit margin can help you decide where to allocate resources.

Fundraising is about mission, as well as money. Put mission first when generating revenue. There are many ways to make money —choose carefully. As executive director, you play a critical role in generating revenue. Embrace it and be an example. Create a culture where fundraising is everybody's job.

People work and give to nonprofits because they want to contribute to something bigger than themselves. This is true of volunteers, including the board, as well as staff. Both paid and unpaid staff need job structure, with clearly defined roles and responsibilities, adequate training, clear and open communication, regular feedback, and opportunities to grow. Tools like Myers-Briggs, Highlands, and DISC improve individual and team success.

Just as one person cannot do it alone, neither can a single agency. As nonprofits, we are part of, and accountable to, our communities. Executive directors must work with their communities. This means collaborating with other agencies, including those with similar missions, complementary missions, similar needs, and similar markets. All these partnerships can improve organizational success.

Strategic planning is a crucial board and executive director function. We laid the foundation in my first year. Executive directors must also be aware of base motivators, how they impact our perspectives and how to make them work for us. We must also recognize both the good and bad consequences of growth.

Know yourself. As a leader, you will define organizational culture. Articulate your values, so everyone in the organization knows what is acceptable and follows the same rule book. Anything you can do to improve your self-awareness is worth the investment. Building your self-esteem will also pay dividends. There are many roads to personal development. Pick yours and embrace it.

Most executive directors aren't good at balancing their personal and professional lives. That balance is important; it keeps you from burning out. Just as with personal values, the quality of your work/life balance will affect organizational success. Schedule time for self-care and develop personal support systems. Despite all the organizational demands, you must take time for self-rejuvenation.

Being an executive director is a big job. You must be proficient in leadership, finance, operations, technology, human resources, resource development, staff development, volunteer management, marketing, and strategic planning. You must have good communication skills, build teams and foster their development, collaborate with others, be insightful, have a high degree of integrity, and share your leadership.

But executive directors don't succeed all by themselves. The nonprofit legal structure demands teamwork. Plus, everyone has strengths and weaknesses. Work off your strengths and surround yourself with people who compensate for your weaknesses. Be vulnerable. Let people know what you need. They want to help. Let them know how they can contribute, be they staff, board, volunteers, funders or community partners. Build your teams and manage them effectively.

I was ready for some of the challenges I faced in my first year —but not all. I hope this book provides insight into becoming an executive director and making it work. Best of luck to you as you make the transition to the executive suite.

Appendix A

Glossary

Assets: Financial term for the value of properties an organization owns, both tangible and intangible. Assets can include cash, stock, equipment, real estate, receivables, and goodwill.

Audit: An examination of records to verify their accuracy. Outside financial audits, required by many funders, are conducted by third-party audit firms.

Board of directors: The body of people with legal and fiduciary responsibility to carry out a nonprofit's mission. An agency's board of directors is ultimately responsible to the public. Also commonly referred to as board of trustees.

Brand: The public's perception of how well an individual, organization or product meets its promises. A nonprofit's brand is the reputation for how, and how well, the agency meets its mission.

Branding: The process of building up an individual's, organization's or product's reputation.

Cash flow: The difference between cash at the beginning of a specific time period and the end of that same period. An accounting of cash coming and cash going out in any given period.

Change agent: A person who alters organizational function to improve output. A person who acts as a catalyst for change.

Corporate culture: The aggregated behaviors, values, beliefs, and characteristics of a corporation or organization.

Culture: The aggregation of behaviors, values, beliefs, and characteristics of a particular social, ethnic, or age group.

Development plan: A fundraising or revenue generation plan.

DISC Assessment: A group of psychological inventories developed by John Geier to measure a person's behaviors. A quadrant behavioral model that examines the behaviors of individuals within their environments.

Ex officio: Holding a position or membership due to the power or influence of one's office or position, rather than by election or appointment.

Executive coach: An experienced, certified individual that specializes in helping executives reach their greatest professional success. Executive coaches emphasize the core drivers and fundamental philosophies that motivate their clients. They help their clients become strong leaders, creative and strategic thinkers, and influential business people.

Executive director: The chief executive officer of a nonprofit. The executive director designs, develops, and implements strategic plans for their organization and manages day-to-day operations. The board grants the executive director authority to manage the organization.

Executive leadership: Leadership at a high organizational level characterized by the abilities to build trust, communicate well, work collaboratively, manage risk, solve problems creatively, influence and inspire others, develop staff and volunteers, and continuously seek improvement.

Feedback loop: A communication mechanism that allows a sender and receiver to adjust and correct their messages based on what is said and what is understood.

Fiduciary responsibility: Holding something in trust for another. Standing in a special relationship of trust, confidence, or responsibility in certain obligations to others.

Governance: The action, manner, or system of making policy and ensuring adherence.

Group dynamics: The processes and emotions that determine interactions in social groups.

Highlands Ability Battery: A series of work samples that measure a person's natural abilities. How easily a person completes a work sample defines how "naturally" the underlying aptitude comes to that person. The Highlands Ability Battery tests for nineteen different abilities.

Internal controls: A coordinated system of procedures and techniques that safeguard a company's assets, ensure the accuracy of its accounting records and promote efficiency and adherence to policies.

Liabilities: Debts or financial obligations.

Management: The responsibility for and control of an organization. The administration of a business or company.

Marketing: The process for creating, communicating, delivering, and exchanging goods or services that have value for donors, funders, clients, partners, and society at large.

Mission: An organization's reason for being. An articulation of what the organization is and why it exists. A mission statement defines who the organization's primary clients are, identifies the products and services the agency offers, and describes the geographical location in which the organization operates.

Myers-Briggs Type Indicator: A psychometric questionnaire designed to measure how people perceive the world and make decisions. The Myers-Briggs Type Indicator is a widely used personality inventory, or test, employed in vocational, educational, and psychotherapy settings to evaluate personality type in adolescents and adults.

Net income: Revenues minus expenses. A positive net income means you have more revenues than expenses. A negative net income means you have more expenses than revenues.

Operating budget: A written budget for the fiscal year, estimating and itemizing all income by sources and all expenditures by project or department. Also called an annual budget or annual operating budget.

Profit margin: A ratio of profitability calculated as net income divided by revenues. It measures how much every dollar of revenue exceeds costs. Profits must be reinvested into the agency's mission, rather than being distributed to owners or shareholders.

Return on investment: A performance measure used to evaluate the efficiency of an investment. Financial return on investment is calculated as net income divided by costs. This metric is useful to compare the financial efficacy of one activity over another. In addition to financial return on investment, nonprofits comparing activities must also take mission return on investment into account.

Revenue structure: A business model. How an organization creates, delivers, and captures economic, social and other forms of value. The model reflects what donors and funders want, how they want it, and how the agency can organize to both meet those wants and get paid for meeting them. How organizational structures are designed to capture different forms of revenue including, organizational purpose, offerings, strategies, infrastructure, business practices, and operational policies and procedures.

Self-care activities: Personal emotional, mental, and physical health maintenance. Any activity to restore health or prevent illness.

Self-esteem: An individual's feelings of self-worth stemming from positive or negative beliefs about their value and capabilities. Personal feelings or opinions towards yourself.

Strategic plan: An organization's written strategy communication intended to achieve the best fit between the organization and its marketplace. A document articulating organizational vision and converting that vision into measurable objectives and performance targets.

Stretch budget: A budget based on goals and ideals rather than previous financial performance.

Vision: A realistic, credible, attractive future for an organization. An articulation of what you want the organization to be.

Work/life balance: The equilibrium people experience when they balance their professional and personal activities.

Appendix B

Recommended Resources

Andresen, Katya. 2008. *Robin Hood Marketing: Stealing Corporate Savvy to Sell Just Causes*. San Francisco, CA: Jossey-Bass.

Barbarto, Joseph. 2005. *Attracting the Attention Your Cause Deserves.* Medfield, MA: Emerson and Church.

Bell, Jean, Jan Masaoka and Steve Zimmerman. 2010. *Nonprofit Sustainability: Making Strategic Decisions for Financial Viability*. San Francisco, CA: Jossey-Bass.

Carlson, Mim and Margaret Donohoe. 2010. *The Executive Director's Guide to Thriving as a Nonprofit Leader (Third Edition)*. San Francisco, CA: Jossey-Bass.

Connor, Tracy D, editor. 2011. *The Volunteer Management Handbook: Leadership Strategies for Success (Second Edition)*. Hoboken, NJ: John Wiley & Sons, Inc.

Crutchfield, Leslie R and Heather McLeod Grant. 2007. *Forces for Good: The Six Practices of High-Impact Nonprofits*. San Francisco, CA: Jossey-Bass.

Daw, Jocelyne. 2006. *Cause Marketing for Nonprofits: Partner for Purpose, Passion and Profits*. Hoboken, NJ: John Wiley & Sons, Inc.

Durham, Sarah. 2010. *Brandraising: How Nonprofits Raise Visibility and Money Through Smart Communications.* San Francisco, CA: Jossey-Bass.

Grace, Kay Sprinkel. 2007. *Fundraising Mistakes that Bedevil All Boards (And Staff Too): A 1-hour Guide to Identifying and Overcoming Obstacles to Your Success.* Medfield, MA: Emerson and Church.

Landsdowne, David. 2004. *The Relentlessly Practical Guide to Raising Serious Money: Proven Strategies for Nonprofit Organizations.* Medfield, MA: Emerson and Church.

Lysakowski, Linda. 2012. *Fundraising for the GENIUS.* Rancho Santa Margarita, CA: For the Genius Press.

Lysakowski, Linda. 2007. *Nonprofit Essentials: The Development Plan.* Hoboken, NJ: John Wiley & Sons, Inc.

McLaughlin, Thomas A. 2006. *Nonprofit Strategic Positioning: Decide Where to Be, Plan What to Do.* Hoboken, NJ: John Wiley & Sons, Inc.

McLaughlin, Thomas A. 2009. *Streetsmart Financial Basics for Nonprofit Managers.* Hoboken, NJ: John Wiley & Sons, Inc.

Olshansky, Norman and Linda Lysakowski, editors. 2011. *You and Your Nonprofit: Practical Advice and Tips from the CharityChannel Community.* Rancho Santa Margarita, CA: CharityChannel Press.

Oppelt, Joanne. 2011. *Confessions of a Successful Grants Writer: A Complete Guide to Discovering and Obtaining Funding.* Rancho Santa Margarita, CA: CharityChannel Press.

Oppelt, Joanne. 2013. *Power Your Organization's Fundraising: How the Partnership Paradigm Will Change Everything.* Rancho Santa Margarita, CA: CharityChannel Press.

Oppelt, Joanne. 2013. *Succeed in Your Nonprofit Funding Partnerships: Analyzing Their Costs and Benefits.* Rancho Santa Margarita, CA: CharityChannel Press.

Index

H

I

J

L

M

N

O

P

W

32600790R00090

Printed in Great Britain
by Amazon